Also by Vince Staten

Ol' Diz

Jack Daniel's Barbecue Cookbook

Unauthorized America

Real Barbecue

Can You Trust a Tomato in January?

Did Monkeys Invent the Monkey Wrench?

Hardware Stores and Hardware Stories

Vince Staten

A TOUCHSTONE BOOK
Published by Simon & Schuster

TOUCHSTONE
Rockefeller Center
1230 Avenue of the Americas
New York, NY 10020

First Touchstone Edition 1997

TOUCHSTONE and colophon are registered trademarks
of Simon & Schuster Inc.

Designed by Deirdre C. Amthor

Manufactured in the United States of America

1   3   5   7   9   10   8   6   4   2

Library of Congress Cataloging-in-Publication Data
Staten, Vince, date.
Did monkeys invent the monkey wrench? : hardware stores
and hardware stories / Vince Staten.
p.   cm.
1. Winfield Hardware.   2. Hardware industry—
West Virginia—Winfield—Anecdotes.
3. Hardware stores—West Virginia—Winfield.
4. Winfield (W. VA.)—Social life and customs.   I. Title.
HD9745.U5W567   1996
381'.45683'0975435—dc20   96-14436
                                            CIP

ISBN 0-684-80132-9
0-684-83274-7 (Pbk.)

For my father, Lyle Staten,
the hardware man in our house
And for Walter Shankel,
the other hardware man in my life

Contents

10   Contents

Chapter 1
Buying Quality Merchandise

RONNIE MATTHEWS COULD FIGURE it out if he needed to. Let's see . . . six days a week, every week since 1978. Subtract two weeks a year for vacation, except that Ronnie didn't take a vacation the first seven years he was in business. But then you'd have to add back in all of the Sundays he came down to open up because someone had called him at home in dire need of a certain size pipe fitting or a particular screw.

At least five thousand times Ronnie Matthews has stuck his key in the front door lock, twisted gently to the left, and opened Winfield Hardware for the day. Sometimes it's just him, turning his back to block the wind.

Sometimes his longtime clerk John Gibson is by his side, ready to follow him inside to sweep the floor and get the place ready for business. And some days there's already a customer hanging around, someone whose pipe busted or toilet overflowed. "Someone with a problem," Ronnie says. "A lot of our business is people in trouble and we've got an answer."

Winfield Hardware isn't just Ronnie Matthews's life. It is Ronnie Matthews. He built it from scratch, less than scratch if you saw his first store, he says.

There's a chill in the air this January day. "Probably won't be selling too many lawnmowers today," Ronnie jokes.

For the 5,212th time Ronnie Matthews is unlocking the door to Winfield Hardware.

It's a scene that's repeated every morning all across America. There are 29,874 hardware stores in this country, some of them bigger than Ronnie Matthews's little outpost in Winfield, West Virginia, some of them smaller.

All of them there to solve a problem. Or two.

Winfield Hardware squats at the corner of Court and Garfield Streets in what might be called downtown Winfield, if there were such a thing.

The business census books describe Ronnie's store as "hardware, retail, 5 to 9 employees, sales less than half a million a year." That's pretty close, says Matthews, except for the employees part. "I've got three, including me."

There are 307 hardware stores in West Virginia, but this is the only one in Zip Code 25213.

This isn't a law office so Ronnie doesn't wear a suit and tie. Today he is decked out in black jeans and a green plaid shirt, topped by a brown leather jacket that he keeps on to cut the chill of a building that was shut down overnight. His pants are hung low in the hardware-store style that was popular long before grunge made the scene.

Ronnie Matthews has been in business eighteen years, and his business philosophy has been the same the whole time. It's a simple philosophy, so simple, in fact, that he has it printed on the back of his business card: "Buying quality merchandise is like buying oats. . . . If you want nice, clean fresh oats, you must pay a fair price. . . . If on the other hand, you want oats that have already been through the horse, then the price would be considerably less."

I will be spending today at Winfield Hardware. That's almost a ten-hour day. Winfield Hardware is open 8:00 A.M. to 5:30 P.M. Monday through Friday and 8:00 A.M. to 5:00 P.M. on Saturday. It's closed Sunday, but as one of the store's regulars, Randy, points out, "If you need something on Sunday, you just call Ronnie and he'll come down and open up for you."

It'll be A Day in the Life of Winfield Hardware but without all the professional photographers swarming around. There'll just be me and Ronnie and his two employees: John Gibson and Ken Garner, "Ken Boy" according to the monogram on his Motion Pizza jacket.

And a lot of hardware.

Ronnie Matthews has been in hardware all his adult life. "I actually started in the hardware business when I was in the ninth grade at Nitro High School. I was the youngest of six and when Daddy went on strike at the locks, I decided if I was going to have any pocket money, I was going to have to earn it."
He went to work at Casto Hardware, a family hardware store in Charleston. "Then I got drafted in 1971. When I come out, I went back to work at Casto—I worked a total of eight years for them."

He quit and worked for a time for Union Carbide. "Then our company went on strike. By the time they called us back, I had decided hardware was what I wanted to be in."

He opened Winfield Hardware in a five-hundred-square-foot building around the curve from his present location. "The day my first son, Ronnie Junior—we call him Duke—was born, I signed the lease for that store. That was June 20, 1978. I started with twenty-five thousand dollars. That wouldn't even get you in the door today."

In 1981 he bought the lot where his store now stands. "I built a five-thousand square-foot building. Three years later I added a four-thousand square-foot addition."

Those years were tight ones financially. "If I sold two

cans of paint, I had to go out and buy two to replace them that night. My supplier was Kanawha Valley Hardware, just down the road, and they were open twenty-four hours. I went out there every night. You could tell who the poor stores were because they were there at midnight buying. And if somebody came in in the day and bought a hot water tank, my wife'd keep 'em busy and I'd run and get it."

The store has been open only a few minutes when the first customer of the day wanders in. Ronnie knows him, as he seems to know most everybody who sidles through the door. And it's not just because Winfield is a small town. "We know most all our customers. It helps if a customer walks in and you can call him by name. They don't get as mad if you're a little high."

And Winfield Hardware is a little high, a little high compared to say Wal-Mart or Home Depot. Ronnie says his markup averages 30 percent. That means if he pays a dollar for an item, he sells it for a dollar thirty.

"Hey there, Stoney," Ronnie smiles to his first customer. He sees the busted part in the man's hand and guesses why he is here. He has a problem. "What size conduit cover you needing? Half-inch?" It's five steps back to the electrical section, two steps over and a short reach into a bin. "This look like it?"

Stoney nods his head.

"Dollar-ninety-eight," Ronnie says, as he taps on the cash register key.

The day has begun.

WHY I'M WRITING THIS BOOK

I've seen guys who could drive a nail in three swings. And not just burly guys, but wiry guys who happened to be very good at hammering.

My brother-in-law Mike Toth can install an electrical outlet without turning off the power. I won't try to unclog the garbage disposal without turning off the power.

My lawn mower man Lew Tabor can diagnose my mower problems over the phone. "Did it squeal?" he asked last time I called because my mower had quit. When I said yes, he shot back, "I can fix that. Bring it in."

I can't do any of those things. I can drive a nail, but it takes me awhile. I can do small repairs. And I can take lawn mowers apart, although I seldom put them back together and have them work any better than they did before.

I am not a repairman.

But I know hardware.

Those guys who can drive a nail in three swings or install an electrical outlet in a heartbeat are craftsmen. They make their livings using tools. They know the whys and hows of construction and repair. I am a weekend warrior and I know my limits.

But I'll bet none of them knows where the monkey wrench came from.

I do. Because I researched it. Because I wanted to know. I'm fascinated by the American preoccupation with tools. And I'm as interested in the guy who thought he could buck the odds and get his new improved lawn trimmer patented and marketed as I am with the Saturday morning handyman who uses that fancy new Weed Eater.

I think that's because I didn't grow up at the elbow of a carpenter. I grew up at the cash register of my father's hardware store.

I was bagging orders before I was tall enough to set them back up on the counter. I was running the cash register at age twelve, handling the stock room at thirteen, waiting on customers at fourteen.

I still have a scar on my knee from an errant linoleum knife.

When I was fourteen and waiting on grizzled old men in work uniforms, I would sell them items I hadn't a clue about. I didn't know what a ballcock did or which was better, copper or aluminum.

But I knew where every item was in my father's store and how much it cost and if there were any accessories that went along with it.

At fourteen I didn't know hardware, but I knew Hardware. I knew the business much better than I knew the stock.

And as I got older, I learned the stock. I picked up the experiences of hardware.

And I learned the people.

Hardware isn't just bagging up pipe fittings and passing them back across the counter to an impatient man whose bathroom is filling up at that moment with water.

Hardware is talking to people about the flash flood down in Rogersville, listening to the story of the commode that exploded or the roof that creaked right before it leaked.

John Kennedy grew up in politics.

Nelson Rockefeller grew up in oil.

I grew up in hardware.

When I was seven years old, my father called the family together to announce that he was leaving his longtime employer, the J. C. Penney Company, to open a hardware store.

I cried. (Of course, I cried every week when Lassie got lost from Timmy.)

I had loved visiting him at Penney's, where I was treated to candy by the candy counter lady, given elevator rides by the elevator lady, and generally treated like a prince. Nobody had ever treated me like a prince when I went with my father to buy something at the hardware store.

For the next thirty years he owned hardware stores in my east Tennessee hometown of Kingsport. He started in a space no bigger than our living room, moved to a store about the size of a small barber shop (today it *is* a barber shop!), then began branching out. At one time he owned four hardware stores and a dime store. In the late sixties he began cutting back. It was too much work, he told me. He closed one store, sold two others, and concentrated on one store, the one at 409 West Sullivan

Street that he had opened in 1959. It was his largest store, and it was only fifty yards from the spot where he had opened his first store. He seemed happy at last.

Hardware was good to me. It bought my bread, financed my college education, and kept me in wheels.

But in the end, I chose not to take over the family hardware empire. I had a different Muse to chase than the one with a hammer and a chain saw.

In 1984 my father locked the door at 409 West Sullivan for the last time. I even have a snapshot of that historic—for our family—moment.

In the years since his downsizing I've married, bought a house, and raised a family of my own. I've repaired lamps, fixed toilets, tiled floors, painted walls, in short, put to use all the different hardware store items that I sold in my youth.

I've put together two tool collections in my lifetime: the first one beginning when I was a kid and lasting until my own children got old enough to use—and lose—tools. The second set has been put together piecemeal. The kids would lose a saw, I would wait until they had moved out of the house to replace it. The result is I still own my first hammer, but I'm on my third saw, my second drill, and what seems like my fifteenth socket set. Those little sockets disappear faster than Oreos in a daycare center.

I was born to write this book.

My wife doesn't understand.

Or perhaps she understands too well.

To her a wrench is just a wrench, a file is just a file, as time goes by.

"Boys and their hammers," she says. And shakes her head.

What is a Hardware Store?

The computer people are trying to steal the name hardware. They use it to refer to the computers themselves, as well as all the little thingies that attach to the computer: scanners and printers and modems and stuff. There is even a chain of computer stores that calls itself The Hardware Store.

I'm not so sure that very many hardware men care. If the word "hardware" blurs into a two-headed monster—"Do you mean tools or computers?"—they'll just begin calling their stores something else. The mammoth stores already seem to prefer the name "home improvement center" for its more modern feeling, but the chains speak often in their corporate communications about "do-it-yourself" items as if they were something different from hardware.

It seems that only the little guys still cling to the name hardware store.

This is a common occurrence in many industries. No sooner had everyone learned what a trailer house was than that industry decided it wanted to to call them mobile homes. Today, that too has given way. If you want to buy a trailer house, look for the fella selling "modular homes."

I have a friend—a retired newspaper man—who served many years on the copy desk of a small-town reactionary rag. His sole joy in life during those miserable years in small-time journalism was taking press releases from the Mobile Home Dealers Association and going through and everywhere it said "mobile home" striking it out and replacing it with "trailer."

I'd hate to see the name hardware store ceded to the computer industry without even a fight. This despite the fact that my father's hardware store never ever had the word "hardware" in its name. It started out as Munford Do-It-Yourself Store and changed, after a breakup of the two partners, to The Do-It-Yourself Center.

The name hardware store has a long and distinguished history, and shouldn't be easily discarded.

The name grew out of the term "hardlines." In the old general store there were three kinds of products: foodstuffs, hardlines, and softlines. Foodstuffs were, uh, food. Softlines were textiles, clothing, and such. Hardlines were metal goods and utensils. Hardline goods were products of substance.

As specialization swept the retail landscape, general stores gave way to grocery stores and department stores and clothing stores and hardware stores.

According to the Oxford English Dictionary, the term "hardware" shows up as early as 1515. A 1723 ad in the *London Gazette* referred to one John Lowe as a "Haberdasher of Hard-Ware." The first use of the term "hardware store" appears in the 1789 *Boston Directory*. Whitwell's is listed as a "hardware store."

So what is a hardware store? It might be easier to begin by knocking out a few things that it isn't.

A hardware store is not just a building. A hardware store doesn't have to be housed in a century-old storefront to qualify. It can be in a brand spanking new shopping center.

And it doesn't have to be old. The floors don't have to creak; the roof doesn't have to leak.

The merchandise doesn't have to be stacked to the ceiling. Spills and stains are not mandatory decor in a hardware store.

Your favorite hardware store may be a century-old storefront with creaking floors and piles of merchandise everywhere, but none of those things are part of my definition of a hardware store. And to find my definition we don't have to turn to the dictionary. We can find it on the streets and side roads of the country.

A hardware store is a collection of smells and sounds. It's a smile and a wink and a handshake. It's an elderly gentleman in an apron and a young boy in a ballcap.

You can't put the hardware-store smell in a bottle; it can't be synthesized and sold as fragrance. Who would buy it if they did? "Ooo, dear, that wonderful aroma . . . what is that?" "It's Hardware Store, honey."

There are components that make up that hardware-store smell. Paint. It's in there somewhere. Used motor oil, from some machinery. Sawdust. Glue—someone is always gluing something in a hardware store. It's all mixed together into an aromatic amalgam that says work. This is where work begins, at the hardware store.

And the sounds of a hardware store: There's hammering in the back, the scratch of glass or ceramic or Formica being scored. There's furniture being shoved around—to get to that item that got tucked behind a counter. And above it all the cash register is singing and in the background there's laughter. The hardware store is a joyful place. It's where folks get together to trade gossip and tell jokes.

Talk, a lot of talk. How to do this, how to change that and take down the other. Along the way stories are swapped like advice. The funniest stories I've heard in my life, I heard in a hardware store.

So what is a hardware store?

A home center is not a hardware store. A home center is too large, too impersonal. It's too much. Home centers are the Disney Worlds of the hardware business. They're breathtaking and fantastic, but no one wants to live at Disney World. Home improvement centers are not hardware stores.

It's not a lumber yard either, although lumber yards may sell many of the same products as hardware stores. Lumber yards are where you buy lumber: big pieces of wood. If you need lumber, you probably need help doing your project. And who has such a good friend anymore that they would help you with a major renovation? For that you have to hire someone. And then you become a contractor. That's what lumber yards are for: contractors.

Hardware stores are for you and for me. They are for running into, picking up a few bolts and a bit of advice.

There are home centers in my town. Lumber yards, too. I go to both of them, but I've never confused either with a real hardware store.

What is a real hardware store?

A real hardware store is a place where you can buy screws by the screw. You don't have to buy a package with some useless number of screws—like seven—in it. Kmart sells screws by the seven. Hardware stores sell screws by the screw.

A real hardware store has everything you need, everything. My father's store had a sign: If we don't have it, you don't need it. Oh, a real hardware store may be out of this item today and that item tomorrow. But they carry faucet washers in a million sizes and nails in a hundred weights. And they can get whatever size or weight or length you need of whatever you need—they'll have it on the next truck. That may not be until next Wednesday, but that's all right. They can get it for you.

And the guys who work in a real hardware store know what they are selling: They've used it, built with it, patched with it, and painted with it.

A real hardware store is a place where they'll offer to

help you with your project if you need it or try to talk you out of it if they think it's going to make you crazy before you're done. A satisfied customer is more important than a sale.

A real hardware store is a place you can call your own. The first time I visited my brother-in-law Powell Toth, way back in 1977, shortly after I got married, he took me on a tour of his little corner of West Virginia. He showed me the college where he taught and the school where the kids went. We visited the state capital and the state museum. And on the way back home he passed a little place called Winfield Hardware. "That's my hardware store," he pointed.

LOCATION, LOCATION, LOCATION

To get to Winfield Hardware, you head north off Interstate 64 on State Route 34. It's a ways, as they say around here. You'll pass Keith's Kitchen and Putnam Seed and Supplies. Once you spot the Cut and Blow Beauty Salon, turn right on U.S. Highway 35.

If you go left, there's Biscuit World, which is a good landmark to note, but it's the wrong direction for hardware.

Drive on past the White House Tavern, which has the most redundant sign I've ever seen in front of a restaurant: "Bikers Welcome." Go under the overpass and there it is on the left, surrounded by Winfield Barber Shop and Wendy's Beauty Salon, just up the street a piece from the

Putnam Democrat newspaper, close to the Fire Department and the IGA, and right across the road from the Highway Patrol.

It's seven miles off the interstate if my odometer is correct.

And with ladders and fertilizer and concrete mix stacked outside, it looks like a hardware store should look.

Winfield Hardware is two blocks from what was once downtown Winfield, but is now Chapman-Erskine Funeral Home and Buster's Sporting Goods and Guns. The Kanawha River is just over the rise, four blocks away.

If you need a piece of pipe or a conduit box in the Kanawha River Valley of West Virginia, this is it. This is the place.

And has been for almost twenty years.

Teay's Valley Hardware is only eight miles away but it might as well be in another county because "it's on the other side of the interstate."

There's a Lowe's Superstore twenty miles away in Huntington, but that's twenty miles and Lowe's, despite its efforts to change its image, is still seen by many around here as a lumber yard.

Hill's, back at the interstate intersection, sells small hardware. So does Hill's neighbor, the Big Bear supermarket.

A-1 Building & Hardware, a Trustworthy Store, is ten miles away in Hurricane.

Winfield Lawn & Tractor is only a mile up the road.

Within a fifteen-mile radius there are lumber yards and discount stores, there's a feed and seed, a lawn mower shop, an appliance store, there are plumbers and carpenters and cabinetmakers and three other hardware stores.

So why is Winfield Hardware still the hardware store of choice in this area? Or for that matter why does anyone buy hardware at a particular store? It's the old real-estate maxim: location, location, location. A 1992 *Hardware Age* survey names "store proximity" as the number-one reason people choose a particular hardware store; 47 percent of folks go to a particular hardware store because it's close. That bodes well for the future of the independent hardware store because no matter how the chains try, they can't build a giant home improvement center on every corner.

The number-two reason people pick a particular store is cost. That was important to 40 percent of the folks surveyed.

Third was product availability: the old "if-they-don't-have-it-at-my-hardware-store-it-doesn't-exist" answer. For 25 percent that reason was reason enough to be loyal.

Math sharpsters will note we are already at more than 100 percent, and there are still two reasons left. That's because people could pick more than one reason for shopping at a store. The number-four reason was knowledgeable sales staff—tabbed by 16 percent. That too bodes well for the little guys. The fifth reason, noted by 9 percent of shoppers, was product quality.

That same survey showed only one-third of shoppers compare prices at other stores before buying.

Hill's has the price advantage. Lowe's has product availability no one else can equal. Winfield Hardware can't touch the big discounters on price. And its nine-thousand square feet wouldn't take up two aisles at Lowe's.

But Winfield Hardware has a knowledgeable sales staff and quality products. And it has location.

And it has one other thing that didn't show up in the survey. It is a hardware store. People like that. Hardware is still purchased predominantly at hardware stores: 41 percent in that same 1992 *Hardware Age* survey. Lumber and building materials centers are second with a 26 percent share. Home centers rank third with 17 percent. Mass merchants—the Wal-Marts and Kmarts—rank fourth at 14 percent.

Until I started work on this book, I had never once considered the location of my father's store. It was where it was, that's all I knew. I'm sure he never did a marketing survey to determine the optimal location for a new hardware store. Hey, he never did any advertising either. When I was a cub reporter and working for the local newspaper, the publisher had a hallway conversation with me about the fact that my father didn't advertise. My response was something to the effect: I don't tell him how to run his hardware business and he doesn't tell me how to write my stories.

As I look back, I'm amazed where he picked for his store. It was in the shadow—and I am talking literally, the shadow—of the warehouse for Dobyns-Taylor, a giant hardware and sporting goods store. And his store was only five blocks from Dobyns-Taylor's large downtown store.

My father located in a strip center: Supermarket Row, it was called, because it had not one, not two, but three supermarkets as its anchors. His store started out one slot from the Little Store supermarket, then moved a hundred yards down, into the middle of the next block, placing it smack between two supermarkets.

There is no synergy between supermarkets and hardware stores. They had their clientele—predominantly female—and my father had his mostly male crowd.

But my father had plenty of parking, something Dobyns-Taylor didn't have in its downtown location. So he had location, staff, product availability, and product quality. He couldn't match price with the big boys, but apparently, he didn't have to.

VINCE MUNFORD

When I was a kid there were some folks who thought my last name was Munford. This was in the days before there was a McDonald's at every intersection. This was when people lent their own names to their stores.

In 1955, when my father opened his first hardware store, the predominant stores in my hometown were

J. Fred's department store, started by the town's founder, J. Fred Johnson; W. B. Greene's dry goods, started by the man who gave it its name and who still lived in town; Fuller and Hillman, a clothing store run by Misters Fuller and Hillman; and Dobyns-Taylor Hardware, again founded by locals and named for them.

The only stores I recall that didn't have local names were well-known national companies: J. C. Penney's, Woolworth's, McCrory's and Kresses.

So it was pretty daring for a local person to open a store under someone else's name. But my father and his partner did. Meade & Staten, Inc., was the owner of Munford's Do-It-Yourself Store.

And that's why some kids called me Munford.

The real Munford was Dillard Munford, an Atlanta entrepreneur who got his start in business as a kid in Cartersville, Georgia, selling pigeons for a dime apiece.

After serving in World War II, he took his four-thousand dollars savings, raised another sixteen-thousand dollars or fifty-thousand dollars, depending on the source, from twelve friends, and opened his first business, a company that manufactured rock wool: insulation, in other words.

In 1951 Munford noticed that contractors weren't the only folks buying his rock wool. Average Joes, weekend handymen, were buying it, too. That's when he got the idea for his first Munford's Do-It-Yourself Store.

The *Oxford Dictionary of the English Language,*

which makes it its business to know these things, says the first use of the expression "do it yourself" was in 1616. It's not exactly "do it yourself" in the context of laying linoleum, but T. Draxe wrote, "If a man will haue his businesse well done, he must doe it himselfe."

The first use in the modern hardware sense—that is, with little hyphens connecting the *do* and *it* and *yourself*—is recorded in a June 30, 1952, article in *Time* magazine about the hardware industry: "Do-it-yourself has brought similar gains, and market shifts, to other industries." Soon the *New York Herald Tribune* was writing about the "tidal wave of do-it-yourselfism" and *The New York Times* was referring to the "do-it-yourselfer" for whom "plywood is as essential as paint, tools, plastics and ordinary lumber." By 1959 we had even exported the word to Great Britain, where the *Manchester Guardian* talked about the "do-it-yourself kit, complete with all necessary screws, bolts, nuts and instruction chart."

The first Munford Do-It-Yourself Store opened in late 1952. "For five years we told people how mysterious it was to put in a floor—and now we tell them anybody can do it," Dillard Munford told *Newsweek.*

Over the next two years Munford opened a total of nine Munford Do-It-Yourself stores with plans to continue opening one a month. He grossed $750,000 in 1954 from all nine stores, with his biggest-selling items plastic floor and wall tile, paint, plywood, and insulation.

His business philosophy was a bit different from that of the average hardware man of the era. "Concentrate on women customers because a man figures 'if a woman can do it, I can do it,'" he told *Newsweek*. He also aimed at the "40-hour a week man with time on his hands."

Of course he didn't "do it himself." He worked eighty hours a week and told *Newsweek*, "I don't have time to do anything around the house."

Shortly after that *Newsweek* article appeared in April 1954, Dillard Munford met my father.

My father wasn't always in hardware. But he was always in sales. He grew up on a farm and was president of his high school's Future Farmers of America chapter, but he never farmed.

It's just as well. He couldn't even grow tomatoes in our backyard. His trials and tribulations at the hands of mail order tomato plants were legend. It was a sad situation: He had all the desire in the world for a gorgeous garden but killed every plant he put his hands on.

So he went into sales, first at The Army Store, a retail shop that specialized in selling surplus military items long before camouflage jackets were chic, then at J. C. Penney's.

By the time I was born in 1947 my father was manager of the shoe department and in line to become assistant store manager. That's when they explained the Penney's way to him. He would be named assistant store manager at a Penney's store in some as yet to be determined location. If his work there were satisfactory, he would get his own store: perhaps in his hometown of Greeneville, Tennessee, perhaps in Greenville, South Carolina, or Greenville, Ohio. Or anywhere. Then he could work his way up the ladder to bigger and bigger stores, moving every two years or so to another town.

That's when he told them he wasn't interested in becoming assistant store manager. Within a few weeks he was moved to the work clothes department.

He learned some hard corporate lessons at Penney's. But he also met the man who would change his life: Ballard Meade.

I don't know why Ballard Meade was working at Penney's at the time because he had an entrepreneur's zeal. He loved starting stores and had done so several times before in his native southwest Virginia.

In 1954 my father borrowed five-thousand dollars on our house—an enormous sum on a house that was built six years earlier for six-thousand dollars—and became the junior half of Meade & Staten, Inc.

They affiliated with the burgeoning Atlanta chain, Munford Do-It-Yourself Stores. At the time do-it-yourself was the rage—vets returning from the war had bought houses and were now tinkering around in them, remodeling, fixing, adding on. It was a postwar phenomenon and Munford, another raging entrepreneur, was trying to capitalize on it.

The price of a Munford franchise was right. There was no franchise fee, only the promise of buying a minimum of one-hundred dollars a month from Munford.

The first Munford Do-It-Yourself Store in my hometown opened at the corner of Dale and Center Streets in a converted grocery store.

Within two years the business had outgrown its humble beginning and was moved to a downtown shopping center. It sat between a barber shop and Rexall Drugs, two doors from The Little Store, a supermarket that belied its name.

For the next three decades, hardware was my father's life. And by extension, my life.

Chapter 2
Tool Department:
Hand Tools,
Power Tools

I WAS IN ONE OF THOSE "building centers" the other day, trying to buy the parts to do a little duct work. I had to stop three clerks before I could find one who could start me on my path. The first pleaded that it was his first day. The second had no excuse.

When I finally grabbed the pipe work that I needed, I started looking for some duct tape. I couldn't find it anywhere, although I did find some reflective tape, two aisles away, which I thought might be even better for my job. But I still wanted to compare it—price and label instructions—to duct tape. So I had to flag down another clerk.

I was now on my fourth clerk.

Duct tape was in paint—of course—along with a second supply of reflective tape.

It made me realize the value of a good clerk but it also made me realize the value of a good store layout.

My father had a good store layout. Ronnie Matthews has a good store layout.

At my father's store—and I admit my memory is skewed toward the end of his store's life—things were arranged logically.

Paint flowed naturally to brushes and thinner and on to cleanup materials. Screws were near wood and metal. Linoleum and tile butted up against adhesives and trim. I'm sure that he didn't figure this out overnight, that it was a gradual process of moving things around. I even remember his partner, Mr. Meade, loved to move things around just for the sake of moving them around. When Mr. Meade was around, no clerk was safe from moving duties.

Winfield Hardware has that same sort of natural flow. Unlike grocery stores, which all seem to begin with produce, hardware stores have no common opening gambit. My father hit you with floor tile, paint, and hand tools. Winfield Hardware has ladders, wood filler, brooms, and bug killer to meet you at the door.

But both stores have a common denominator: They both put popular items at the back. With Winfield Hardware it's plumbing supplies. Ronnie says they are his biggest sellers. My father put rental tools in the back of his store, along with another popular item, wood stain. I remember suggesting to him once that he move the rental tools to the front so people who came in just to rent a tool wouldn't have to walk the length of the store. I told this story to Ronnie and he said, "I bet I know what he told you. He told you, 'I don't want them just to rent a tool.'"

That's why bread and milk are in the back of the grocery. And that's why popular items are in the back of the hardware store.

They don't want you to come in for just one item.

STANLEY 16-OUNCE GRAPHITE HAMMER—$22.98

If you've seen the movie *2001: A Space Odyssey* you remember the opening scene: It's the dawn of time. An apeman invents the first tool, a bone club he uses to clobber members of a rival group that is battling his clan over a Stone Age water hole.

I think I've witnessed that same scene in Sears on a Saturday morning, when there is only one gallon of Weatherbeater White left on the shelf.

There was a time when there was no Sears; no True Value Hardware; no Black, no Decker. In short, no tools.

If you're thinking "and probably no men either," you're almost correct. There were men—and women— but if you were to meet our early ancestors at the hardware store today, you might recoil. They were short, stooped, hairy, missing-link-looking hominids with sloped foreheads and gargantuan Nancy Kerrigan teeth.

These early humans have been named the *Robust Australopithecines* by anthropologists, and they roamed the grasslands of east and south Africa about 2.6 million years ago. These early ancestors had small brains, because, frankly, they didn't need large brains. Oprah wasn't on yet. And those giant teeth were part of nature's natural selection. They needed large teeth and massive jaws to grind up the tough, fibrous plants that composed the bulk of their diet.

Soon—if you consider two-hundred-thousand years soon—these little men and little women were joined in the food chain by another evolving species we now call *Homo habilis*. These guys had larger brains, smaller teeth, and a diet that didn't require nonstop chewing. Archaeologists tell us these early hominids probably evolved from a different species than *Robust Australopithecines*. At this late date, we just don't know.

What we do know is that it was *Homo habilis*—the big-brain boys—who discovered tools, and not the duncecap ancestors.

Now discovering tools was not nearly as easy for these Stone Age ancestors as, say, discovering fire. A little lightning, a little dry grass and—voilà!—fire.

But there weren't little band saws and nut drivers lying around under rocks, waiting for a caveperson to turn over the right rock.

Tools were invented—that's a better word for it than

discovered—as a result of these early humanesque crea-
tures' desires to control their environment rather than
be controlled by it.

Scientists believe the first tool was a hammer, a very
primitive hammer. Our cave-friend Og found a rock and
hit another rock with it, resulting in either rock chips or
a sore hand. These rock pieces could then be used for
other purposes.

The chips that these Stone Age tool guys managed to
flake off their rocks had different uses, but all of them
involved survival, which at the time was more important
than, say, adding a deck to the cave.

Some rock chips were used for throwing, either as of-
fensive weapons or to ward off an enemy, not that peb-
bles could forestall a saber-toothed tiger from a sure
meal. Others were used for cracking open nuts to liber-
ate the meaty centers. Still others were suited for bone
crushing, so hungry Og could eat the marrow. Rock
pieces, depending on the size and shape, were also used
for digging, for butchering animals, for working animal
hides into usable material, and even for woodworking,
although not to cut out a little armoire for the missus.

After a while Og learned to select his hammer stone
carefully. From archaeological diggings, we know the
earliest preferred shape was the egg-shaped or oblong
rock. It didn't cut into the hand of the hammer-wielder
as a jagged rock would and it was easier to use. We can't
be certain exactly when caveman or cavewoman first hit
rock on rock, but from fossil evidence we can date it at

about 2.4 million years ago—give or take a couple of weeks.

Charles Darwin—the guy who discovered the theory of evolution—proposed that tool use was one of the primary reasons the first humans walked upright: to free the hands to carry things and use tools. In *The Ascent of Man* he postulated that walking upright was selected by evolution: "They would thus have been better able to defend themselves with stones and clubs, to attack their prey or otherwise obtain food."

But Kathy Schick, an Indiana University anthropologist, says the current thinking is there is no evidence that the first bipedal hominids used tools. At least none are preserved with their fossils. Man had already stood erect before inventing the hammer. Inventing the hammer was a good idea; standing erect was a better one.

Which is not to downplay the invention of tools.

Tools changed the entire course of human civilization.

Schick says that because we took the technological path, the tool path, we developed as we did. Otherwise we might still be wandering the Serengeti, making goofy bird sounds, trying to lure other animals within range of our rock-throwing abilities. And how good would Oprah be at that?

Even if we don't know to the day when the hammer came along, we do know that it was then—and still is now—the first tool every man needs and the one he uses most. If you're in the market for a new hammer, Ronnie advises against buying one with a fiberglass handle. "A lot of carpenters won't buy fiberglass. They like metal or wood. They say when you pound with it all day fiberglass vibrates up in your arm and wears you out."

SNAP-ON 14-INCH MONKEY WRENCH—$25.98

In the 1930s Robert Ripley, author of the widely syndicated—and wildly popular—reality comic strip "Ripley's Believe It or Not," proclaimed in his strip that the monkey wrench was invented by British mechanical whiz Charles Moncke, a blacksmith. The big boys of word origins—the *Oxford Dictionary* people—picked up on the story and that has been common wisdom ever since. But it flies in the face of etymological logic: the British don't call it a monkey wrench. They use the name "adjustable spanner wrench."

When I first began work on this book, I thought that the monkey wrench really did get its name from monkeys. After all, many tools get their names from their appearance. The crane is so named because it resembles a crane's neck. And if you hang a monkey wrench handle down it does look like a monkey.

As it turns out, the monkey wrench is as American as monkey business, a slang term we invented to describe foolishness (like trying to figure out who invented and named the monkey wrench).

Monkeys really did invent the monkey wrench.

Well, a monk: Mr. Monk of Springfield, Massachusetts.

This Monk fellow was a mechanic in the Springfield machine shop Bemis & Call. According to Addison Lincoln, whose father took over the company in 1935— "He was hired by the last Mr. Bemis"— Monk invented the movable jaw for a wrench back in 1856. At first it was referred to simply as an adjustable wrench, but workers in the shop started calling it Monk's Wrench. Monk's Wrench soon became vulgarized to "monkey wrench."

"That's one version of how it got its name," says Lincoln. "There are actually two stories."

The other story has a later origin. "It happened when my father was here in the thirties. He said there was a guy working with this type wrench and he told the other fellows in the shop, 'Don't monkey around with my wrenches.'"

Lincoln says the official version is that the monkey wrench owes its existence to a guy named Monk.

"But my father always told me it was a guy whose name wasn't Monk who gave the monkey wrench its name."

I found a third version in an 1886 article in the Springfield, Massachusetts, *Daily Union*. An earlier article had claimed that the inventor of the monkey wrench was Springfield native son Charles Monckey, who sold his invention and moved to Williamsburg, New York. This flew in the face of common wisdom at Bemis & Call. Amos Call, president at the time, sent a letter to Monckey asking for details on this invention. Monckey never replied and Call took his case to the local newspaper. He told reporter M. S. Robinson his version of the story: In 1840 local machinist Solymon Merrick fashioned a primitive version of the monkey wrench. He took his unsatisfactory invention to a Mr. King of nearby Chicopee. King suggested an improvement, Merrick made the change, and the monkey wrench was born. If not the name.

Merrick took his wrench back to his shop and began manufacture. His principal workman on the wrench was a man by the name of White, who, according to Robinson, "because of an unprepossessing personal appearance was known to his shopmates by the nickname of 'Monkey.'"

To differentiate the wrench that White was working on from the wrenches they were manufacturing, the other workers took to calling it Monkey's wrench.

This was pretty much an in-house nickname for many years. The 1886 directory *Leading Mass. Industries and Merchants of Central & Western Mass.* includes a laundry list of wrenches manufactured by Bemis & Call, but none are designated "monkey wrench."

So who really did invent the monkey wrench?

Charles Moncke? Mr. Monk? Solyman Merrick and Mr. King? "Monkey" White? If I had to pick, I'd go with the Monkey White story, simply because it's the oldest tale.

But really all these conflicting tales do is throw a monkey wrench in the works.

STANLEY 12-INCH CENTER SCREW WRENCH—$18.98

You may have heard this variation on the monkey wrench called a "King Dick" wrench. You may have thought it was a slur on the person using it: some officious type who considered himself King Dick. Actually the King Dick Company was the original manufacturer, although I prefer almost any story about how it got its name to the truth.

AMES LONG-HANDLED ROUND SHOVEL—$19.98

If it weren't for the American Revolution, you might be shopping at Ye Olde Hardware Shoppe instead of a hardware store. You see the British, who owned us lock, stock, and barrel bolt until the Revolution, forbade manufacturing in their colonies. The colonies were created as markets for British goods.

So Captain John Ames was committing treason when he began fashioning shovel blades from wrought iron in 1774.

Fortunately for him the Revolution was just around the corner.

In the years before the American Revolution all American-made shovels were wooden. Only British imports were made of metal. Enter Ames, a Bridgewater, Massachusetts, blacksmith who in 1774 founded the Ames Company to correct that. Using an eighty-pound water-powered trip-hammer he shaped his shovels out of iron bars. He sold them with the claim that the competition, the wooden shovel, "didn't destroy the earth but were destroyed by the earth."

That makes Ames the oldest brand-name manufacturer in the hardware business, because Ames was making shovels a full year before Paul Revere's ride.

In the beginning, Ames employed his neighbors, most of whom were farmers, in the winter months between the October harvest and the May planting. It took twenty people to make a shovel then: heating it in the fire, pounding it into shape, reheating, reshaping, testing the weight, the balance, the durability. You could make a musket about as easily as you could make a shovel. Of course a shovel was more valuable—you used it to till the soil and raise your provisions—at least until the war broke out.

After the war hundreds of small manufacturing plants sprang up all over the New England states and wasn't that an ironic name for the area, New England?

The biggest boost to American manufacturing came from Eli Whitney, who in 1799 began manufacturing flintlocks from interchangeable parts. No more one-of-a-kind items, right, but also no more one-of-a-kind prices.

The earliest manufacturers in this country were Borden, Cooper, Disston, Gilbert & Bennett, Harger, McKay-Empire, Oldham, Simonds, Stanley, and True Temper.

The seminal moment in shovel history was the invention by Ames of what is now called the Ames bend. Before Ames all shovel handles were straight as a poker. This now well-known bend made a shovel balanced and more comfortable to use. The Ames bend allowed users to stand at a more comfortable angle and use the shovel more naturally. And it was John Ames who saw the problem and created a solution.

The other great advancement in shovel history was the tempering of blades. This allowed thinner, easier-to-use blades, and the tempering added flexibility, which reduced breaking.

You'd never know it from watching *How the West Was Won* or any of the Way West movies, but the shovel was what won the West. The shovel was so instrumental in the building of the railroads that companies would put out booklets commemorating the shovels that dug the trenches instead of the laborers whose backs were sore from building the transcontinental railroad. These booklets would detail a particular shovel's days, months, and years in service, sometimes even noting mileage!

Today there are over one thousand different kinds of shovels, including the coffee bean shovel, the telegraph spoon shovel, and the ceremonial shovel (used for ground-breaking ceremonies).

And Ames is the world's largest manfacturer of shovels.

One shovel should last you a lifetime. Unless you do what I did, which is back over ours with the car. Okay, who left it in the driveway? I made mincemeat of the handle, but the shovel itself was unscathed.

With replaceable handles, my back will probably

wear out before my shovel. Although I'm working on that. I take the advice of Bethlehem Steel, which conducted extensive studies to determine the optimal load for a shovel. Bethlehem concluded it was twenty-one pounds. If you don't put more than twenty-one pounds in the shovel spoon you shouldn't be troubled by strain or fatigue. Since I don't know exactly what twenty-one pounds of dirt looks like, I make sure my load is always under it.

STANLEY RECIPROCATING SAW — $17.98

What? Saws reciprocate? Does this mean that saws live by the Golden Rule, that they do unto others as they would have others do unto them?

No, this means the saw has a reciprocating part: a part that moves back and forth. There have been reciprocating saws since the middle of the nineteenth century.

STANLEY COPING SAW — $12.98

The coping saw isn't so named because it's just barely getting by. The name comes from the craft of masonry, in which the coping is a sloping of the brickwork that throws off the rain. It's curved. So when saws were invented in the late nineteenth century to cut curving patterns, they were naturally called coping saws, because they cut in a coping pattern.

HAMPE MITER BOX—$26.98

I always thought the miter box somehow derived its name from the word meter—you know, the unit of measurement in use everywhere in the world except here, the one they keep threatening to unleash on America because our foot-yard-mile-acre-quart system is only good for measuring things like football fields.

I was wrong. The term "miter" also comes from masonry. A miter was a forty-five-degree angle joint. Today a miter box is used to cut forty-five-degree angles. Take two boards cut at a forty-five-degree angle, joint them together and you will produce a right angle. Two miters equal a right angle. Two meters equal 6.5616 feet. Got it?

BLACK & DECKER ⅝-INCH POWER DRILL—$53.98

Their names are as familiar to men as Ruth and Gehrig, Smith and Wesson, Bartles and Jaymes. But who *were* Black & Decker?

Black was Duncan Black, a Baltimore tool-and-die cutter, who in 1910 joined with his longtime friend and fellow tool-and-die cutter Alonzo Decker to open a machine shop. Using the six-hundred dollars Black got from selling his car, and a twelve-hundred-dollar bank loan, they rented a warehouse on Calvert Street in downtown Baltimore and opened their doors for business.

The first few years of the existence of Black & Decker, Inc., were uneventful. The two mostly did what they had been doing before—making tools—only now they were the ones making the money, instead of their bosses. They made a postage-stamp-splitting and -coiling machine for the government, a milk-bottle-cap maker for a local dairy, a cotton picker, a vest-pocket adding machine, even a candy-dipping machine.

The seminal moment for Black & Decker came in 1914 when Black came up with a new idea for the power drill. Before then most power tools were German-made, heavy and difficult to operate. The power drill was especially cumbersome. It was designed like a screwdriver and it kept slipping out of the worker's hand. Black took his cue from the Colt revolver and designed an electric drill with a pistol grip and a trigger switch that operated on the same principle as the gun's trigger. They took the half-inch pistol-grip electric drill to market in 1916—along with the since-forgotten Lectroflater air compressor. And drills haven't been the same since.

In the eight decades since that invention, Black & Decker has introduced hundreds of other power tools, from the circular saw to the electric screwdriver.

But it is that drill, and that drill alone, that made Black and Decker household names. In 1919, only three years after introducing the pistol-grip electric drill, Black & Decker, Inc., was doing a million dollars a year in sales. They made more money than Babe Ruth that year because they had a better year.

Black and Decker weren't just a couple of muscled-up rubes who hit on a good idea. They knew what to do with a good idea once they had one. In 1925 they bought two Pierce Arrow school buses and sent them around the country, demonstrating the company's lines to salesmen and plant operators. In fact in 1929, the year Wall Street collapsed, Black & Decker expanded. The company bought a Massachusetts company that made wire wheel brushes, hole saws, and grinding stones.

And if you think it a bit silly today when you see the Black & Decker brand on a hair dryer or a waffle iron, it's nothing new. Black & Decker first entered the housewares market in 1930 with the since-forgotten Black & Decker Cinderella washing machine.

But despite all its innovations and products, its patents and trademarks—the Shorty drill, the Holgun drill, the LectroShear metal cutter, the Lawnderette electric lawn mower, the Workmate portable work bench, the VersaClutch air screwdriver, the Dustbuster cordless vacuum among them—the reason folks today know Black & Decker is a decision the company made in 1946.

Before there even was a Munford Do-It-Yourself Store, Black & Decker decided to enter the home do-it-yourself market. In 1946, the company introduced a low-priced line of portable tools. If you bought any power tools in the fifties you remember the brand name: Home-Utility. The Home-Utility ¼-inch portable electric drill—priced at $16.95—was the first portable electric drill designed for consumers and not contractors. In the first five years of its manufacture the company sold one-million of the little drills. I'll bet my father sold a thousand of them over the years. Ronnie says it's been one of his best sellers. And there are probably ten stores within easy driving distance of Winfield Hardware that sell them: from Lowe's to the discount stores.

Black & Decker today is run by corporate managers, professional businessmen, who were hired into the company. But the two men responsible for Black & Decker's spectacular growth and popularity were the two men who lent it their names. Duncan Black and Alonzo Decker ran the company from its founding in 1910 right through the postwar do-it-yourself boom. Duncan Black died in 1951, Alonzo Decker in 1956. As recently as 1975, when Alonzo Decker, Jr., gave up the title of CEO, a family member was still running the company. (He retired as chairman of the board in 1979.)

Today the company makes so many products in so many countries that it would take an entire chapter just to list them all.

Maybe Duncan Black and Alonzo Decker are not as famous as Ruth and Gehrig, but in a 1989 survey of ten-thousand brand names, Black & Decker ranked seventh. They may not have a baseball card, but they really knew how to play the hardware game.

BLACK & DECKER CHUCK KEY — $2.98

This isn't the Ford ignition key that fell out of Chuck's pocket when he went to get his billfold. This is the little screwdriverlike tool that you use to tighten the drill's chuck around the bit.

It isn't named for anyone named Chuck.

Originally the part that held the bit on a tool was called a chock. The British, with their bad teeth, pronounced chock and chuck the same way, so apparently the friendly colonists thought it was that Chuck guy's name.

Ronnie says chuck keys are a thing of the past. "Next time you buy a drill get the self-chucking kind. That's the way to go."

DEWALT ¼-INCH DRILL BIT — $2.49

Consider the lowly drill bit.

The drill bit gets so little respect that when we can't locate a bit at our house—if you have children, you know what I am talking about—we substitute a nail. A finishing nail works just fine for drilling a small hole into wood.

But the drill bit is a mechanical marvel.

Different-shaped bits have different uses. Auger bits are for deep holes; Forstner bits for large shallow holes; countersink bits for beveled holes.

There are bits for wood, bits for metal, and bits for masonry.

And if you think all drill bits are created equal, talk to Howard Hughes. Okay, you can't; he's dead. But his fortune—and he was so rich he didn't even bother buying lottery tickets—came from the drill bit.

His father, the wildcat oil man Bo Hughes, built his first fortune by buying oil-rig drill-bit patents. He blew that fortune in a poker game and started over. This time he invented his own drill bit, basing his design on the ribbing on the butter pats he was served in a Louisiana saloon. By 1918 his invention—the Hughes tool bit—was perfected and was being sold all over the world.

The son built on the father's empire and eventually owned most of Las Vegas as well as a silly spruce-pine airplane. When he died in 1975 Howard Hughes was acknowledged as the richest—and strangest, but that's another story—man in the world. A massive fortune based on the drill bit.

IRWIN AUGER DRILL BIT—$5.98

If you thought Irwin Auger was a character on the old *Huckleberry Hound* cartoon show, well, it sounds like he should be.

Actually there is no Irwin Auger, the person. But there is an Irwin Auger drill bit.

It's a solid bit that's been around for more than a century. And it owes its existence to whiskey and the business acumen of an Ohio pharmacist.

The druggist was Charles Irwin, who ran Irwin's Drugs in Wilmington, Ohio. In the 1880s whiskey was sold in drugstores as well as saloons, and one of Irwin's best whiskey customers was the village smithy, William Dimmit. Dimmit lived up to his surname: He was dim. He ran up a whiskey bill and then was unable to pay. So he offered Irwin a deal. Erase his whiskey debt and he would give Irwin the process he had developed for making solid auger drill bits.

Deal, Irwin said. He immediately patented Dimmit's process, signed on four other businessmen, and in 1885 opened the Irwin Auger Bit Company on a ten-thousand-dollar investment. They hired the flamboyant General James Denver, the man for whom the Colorado city would be named, and they were off. By the turn of the century Irwin Auger was the world's largest producer of wood-boring tools.

Today the company is run by Graves Williams, Jr., grandson of, you guessed it, James Denver.

THORSEN ½-INCH DRIVE 15-PIECE SOCKET SET— $6.59

I don't remember my father selling socket sets in the fifties and sixties, the years I worked for him. It was not the ubiquitous shade-tree-mechanic necessity then that it is today. In fact I don't even remember seeing socket sets back then. I don't remember when I first saw one.

My friend Bruce Haney remembers the first socket set he saw.

"Brownie Williams and a bunch of us were coming

back from the beach in 1964 and we were about to run out of gas. We stopped at a gas station somewhere in South Carolina and stripped the car looking for something to sell. Finally the guy agreed to trade us gas for a socket set they found in the trunk."

(Incidentally, Bruce's mother is hearing this story for the first time right here.)

The socket set was in existence before 1964 but it wasn't until about that time that it went from optional to required in tool boxes. And that change occurred with a change in the socket set itself. It went from clumsy tool to jackrabbit-quick handy tool with the invention in 1964 of the quick-release ratchet wrench. Before, you just turned the driver to turn the socket. You turned it and turned it, round and round and round.

We owe this hardware-history-shattering event to an eighteen-year-old kid who was tinkering around in his dad's garage.

The kid's name was Peter Roberts, and we might never have heard of him if he hadn't had to sue Sears to collect his rightful due. Sears had paid Roberts a mere ten-thousand dollars when it purchased his invention in 1965.

Roberts grew up in Gardner, Massachusetts, an hour west of Boston. His dad was a furniture factory superintendent who earned pocket money repairing lawn mowers.

Socket sets were in common use in 1964—a socket was an easy way to grip a nut—as were ratchet wrenches, which allowed you to turn a bolt without making a full circle with the socket arm. That year Roberts, who was a junior at Gardner High School, took an after-school job at Sears, working as a clerk, cashier, and janitor. After graduation, he stayed on full time.

Working with his dad on lawn mowers, he became convinced that a one-handed ratchet wrench, one that had a button to release the socket from the wrench's grip, was what the world needed.

He'd never taken mechanical drawing so his design didn't conform to standard mechanical thinking. It was asymmetrical. He made one up in his dad's shop—his dad was always fashioning tools to help in lawn mower repair—and to his astonishment it worked.

So in May of 1964 Roberts took his homemade wrench to Edward Lemeux, his boss at Sears, and asked him what he should do with it. After all, it worked. Lemeux submitted it to the muckety-mucks in Chicago, and when he didn't get an immediate acceptance Roberts assumed that was the last he would hear. Sears actually closed the Gardner, Massachusetts, store at the end of that month.

Soon thereafter the Roberts family moved to Red Bank, Tennessee, a small town just outside Chattanooga.

The wheels were turning in Sears corporate offices. The wrench was impressive and Sears designated attorney Leonard Schram to negotiate with now-nineteen-year-old Roberts.

It was January 1965. Roberts was working at Overholtz Hardware store in Newport, Tennessee, when he got a phone call. Schram asked for the name of the attorney who was handling Roberts's patent application. It was a small-town guy back in Massachusetts, Roberts said. A guy named Charles Fay of Worcester, Massachusetts. Roberts wondered about the status of his wrench and Schram replied, cryptically, "Sometimes inventors get more for their ideas than they are really worth."

Schram got in touch with Fay and they quickly made a deal: Roberts would get a royalty of two cents per wrench sold with the quick-release feature. After all, it would cost Sears nearly forty cents to add the button and assembly to the wrench. There was one catch. The royalty was for a maximum of fifty-thousand wrenches, about half the number Sears was currently selling a year. Of course there was no guarantee that this new-style wrench would take off, Schram advised. Still it was only two cents per wrench.

In a letter Fay explained the deal to Roberts, advising him, "Perhaps it would be better for you to go along with his idea." By the time Roberts got the contract on June 15, 1965, Sears was buying worldwide patent rights. Roberts signed, even though he was legally a minor. It was a bird in the hand. Sears led Roberts to believe it might be ten years before he would earn his full royalty amount: ten thousand dollars. Instead, on September 22, 1966, a little over a year later, Roberts received a check for the full amount. He was in the Air Force in England and balked at cashing the check. But when he could find no suitable legal advice, he deposited it. Hey, wouldn't you? When he returned to the United States in January 1969, he immediately hired a lawyer, Louis Davidson of Chicago. Before the calendar year was over, Davidson had filed a fraud suit against Sears.

At the time Sears was selling about a million ratchet wrenches a year under its well-regarded Craftsman brand. To be exact—and court records are nothing if not exact—Sears sold 1,153,359 in 1964. Ten years later, in 1975, they sold 2,805,867.

The population didn't grow that rapidly in that decade so you have to attribute some of the sales increase to Roberts's handy-dandy invention. And the courts did.

When all the legal dust had settled, the court ruled that Sears owed Roberts more, much more. Like a million bucks. Plus, Sears had to give him his patent back.

Today Roberts is selling a new-type socket wrench set; he calls it the Dynamo Socket Wrench. You may have seen the TV ads; he's selling it through an 800 number.

I don't have one, although I'm sure it's a swell new tool. It's just that this is a book about hardware stores, not infomercials.

7-INCH VISE-GRIP—$10.95

The strangest-looking tool in your basic tool box has to be the Vise-Grip.

These locking pliers, which can be used as pliers, as a wrench, as a vise, or as a clamp, were invented in 1920 by Danish immigrant William Petersen of DeWitt, Nebraska.

Petersen, a blacksmith by trade, devised the locking vise wrench to help in repairing farm machinery and the Model T Fords that were finding their way into his blacksmith shop. He needed a small, portable vise in his work so he whittled one out of wood.

That's right: The first Vise-Grip was wooden. It worked, but it soon became apparent to Petersen that wood was not the way to go. So he began hand-forging his tool, each time making a slight improvement.

In 1924 Petersen actually took a train from eastern Nebraska to Washington to get his invention patented.

That first Vise-Grip allowed the handyman to lock whatever he was working on between a fixed and a movable jaw. The movable jaw was adjusted by a bolt built into the handle. New since he first began tinkering with his Vise Grip was a toggle-locking lever.

Petersen began manufacture of these handy vise tools and was soon employing his entire family.

His sons traveled to county fairs, selling Vise Grips out of the trunk. Their sister stayed back home and kept the books.

Sales of the Vise-Grip really took off after World War II. American GIs sold the rest of the world on the Vise-Grip when they used them to repair bunks, guns, Jeeps, even airplanes during the war.

The last major improvement to the Vise-Grip came in 1957 with the addition of the easy-touch toggle release lever.

Today Petersen Manufacturing sells millions of Vise-Grips a year, despite the fact that other manufacturers have competing models. The Vise-Grip is available in a half-dozen lengths from four to ten inches and with a variety of jaws suited to a whole host of jobs. They are still manufactured in the town where they were invented, DeWitt, Nebraska by the original company. And it's still a family enterprise. The company is run by Allen Petersen, grandson of William Petersen.

STIHL 20-INCH CHAIN SAW — $259.98

Once the rite of passage from boyhood to older boyhood was when your dad took you out and taught you how to shoot a gun, but the migration from the country to the city and then back out to the suburbs has changed the ritual. No longer can a man show his son the rudiments of riflery without the risk of taking out a satellite dish or a drain gutter.

Today there's a new rite of passage: It's when your dad takes you out and shows you how to use a chain saw.

On any Saturday morning in the suburbs you can hear the buzzing of chain saws, scores of hand-held ripsaws that make it sound as if the subdivision is about to take off.

The chain saw has its roots in woodcutting, a skill that is as old as mankind. Pioneers, who had a whole lot of forests to clear, were using chains to move saw blades as early as 1770. But the chain saw as we know it isn't that old. The first step toward a chain saw came in the late 1800s when sawmills first used electricity to help power their saws. In 1904 Jacob Smith of Des Moines, Iowa, invented a crank-start semiportable woodcutting machine. The next year, 1905, the Ashland Iron Works in Oregon developed a similar product that operated on compressed air.

The first real development in chain saw history came in 1910 when R. L. Muir of Redlands, California, invented a saw that cut wood with a moving toothed chain. The difference between Muir's "chain saw" and the modern device was in the power train: Muir's saw was driven by a large machine mounted on a cart. It required a crane to lift and power the cutting bar. Muir's invention was a technical success but a commercial failure.

American inventor Charles Wolf devised an electric-powered woodcutting machine in 1911, but it took an entire crew to operate it. And a very long cord, making it of little use in the woods. So it still wasn't a chain saw.

The invention of the chain saw was left to a German repairman named Andreas Stihl, who lived in Stuttgart, near the Black Forest. Stihl was a loafer by avocation and he frequently strolled the forest, watching loggers perform their backbreaking work. In a nearby tavern

Stihl befriended the loggers and listened to their tales of woe concerning their inadequate power saws. He helped repair the woodcutting machines, which didn't work very well to begin with. As one machine broke and was replaced by a newer, larger, heavier model, Stihl got an idea. The power-saw manufacturers were going in the wrong direction. Loggers didn't need bigger power saws, they needed smaller ones.

In 1926 Stihl patented the "Cutoff Chain Saw for Electric Power." It was like the modern chain saw in almost every way: It looked like a chain saw, ran like a chain saw, even cut wood like a chain saw. But it used an electric motor, tying loggers to an electrical outlet, something that just wasn't there in the deep forest.

The next year he improved his invention with the addition of a gasoline engine. He was almost there. There was still one remaining problem: Stihl's Midget Cutoff Chain Saw wasn't much of a midget. It weighed 127 pounds. That might have been okay for Arnold Schwarzenegger, but he hadn't been born yet. By 1931 Stihl had pared twenty-three pounds off his original creation. Now it was just a matter of time. He began experimenting with lightweight alloys, improved guide bars, more efficient cutting chains. By 1936 Stihl chain saws weighed a mere—if *mere* is the word—forty-seven pounds and he was the world leader in chain-saw production.

A decade later Joe Cox of Portland, Oregon, would devise improved chain cutters. In 1949 the McCulloch company developed a smaller, more powerful motor. But the chain saw owes its existence to one man, Andreas Stihl. That's why I will never buy another brand. A Stihl chain saw pays homage to the man who saw the future of woodcutting, and his name was Stihl.

CASE KNIFE—$6.98

When I was a kid, you weren't a boy unless you carried a pocketknife. None of us considered it a weapon except for Butch Deaton, who thought everything was a weapon. A pocketknife was a tool. You could use it to cut string, peel an apple, open a letter, tighten a screw, and—if you were the prissy type—clean your fingernails.

Now the pocketknife has gone the way of the pocket watch.

Ronnie says he still carries them at Winfield Hardware but they don't sell the way they once did. He has his ensconced in a case on the end of an aisle. "A lot of knives have been stolen over the years in hardware stores."

He has them in a case so they are case knives, right?

My father carried what we always called case knives. We thought they were case knives because he sold them out of a locked case. Case knives were the only item in my father's entire store that we kept locked up. (Well . . . later he would lock up Solox, but that's another story—and that story's on page 139.)

It was only in later years that I learned they were called case knives because of the Case brand.

My father didn't sell Case brand and neither does Winfield Hardware (Ronnie sells Buck and Saber brands), but, just the same, many folks still call them case knives. I'm not sure if they know it's because of Russ Case and not because they are in a case.

Case knives date to the late nineteenth century and the founding in Little Valley, New York, of the W. R. Case & Sons Cutlery company. That area is the center of what knife aficionados now call the Magic Circle, an area with a one-hunded-mile diameter that is home to many cutlery companies. J. Russell "Russ" Case named his company after his father, William Russell Case. In 1905 Russ built a factory in Bradford, Pennsylvania, and that is still home to case knives.

The way to tell a real case knife is to check the blade for the famous XX trademark. That distinguishing mark came from Case Brothers Cutlery Company, a cousin's firm. Russ Case purchased the XX trademark in 1911, after Case Brothers was destroyed by fire

Actually the double X is more than just a trademark, it's the cutlery equivalent of "inspected by." It seems the best knife blades are hardened with two heat treatments in a furnace. Originally the blade containers were branded with an x after each heating, thus a knife that was ready for market would have XX.

That double X became recognized as a mark of quality. And, in the process, Case became synonymous with the pocket knife.

The company has never advertised, preferring to let the knife speak for itself. Case did do one thing to distinguish itself from the competition. It began offerring dealers a fine crafted display case—the other *case* of case knives. Stores snapped them up, and in 1935 the company even built a cabinet shop just to keep up with the demand for Case cases.

Today Case knives are still the first choice of collectors. And that's about all that buys them. Little boys sure don't.

SWISS ARMY KNIFE—$6.98

One of my kids wanted a Swiss Army knife for Christmas. Until that moment, I had never even thought about the Swiss Army knife. But as I wrapped the knife, I got to thinking: Do members of the Swiss Army carry Swiss Army knives? And—hey—why does a neutral country like Switzerland need an army? So how could there be a Swiss Army Knife?

The truth is there really is a Swiss Army. But it's not a fierce fighting unit. "It's just for defensive purposes," according to a spokeswoman for the Swiss Embassy in Washington, D.C. And those stalwart defenders really do carry Swiss Army knives. "It's a very popular item." And they have been carrying them for over a century.

The Swiss Army knife got its start in 1891 when Swissman Karl Elsener found out that the official knives supplied to Swiss Army recruits were made in Germany, of all places! He developed a wooden-handled pocketknife that also contained a screwdriver, a can opener, and a punch and sold the Swiss Army on his invention, which he called the soldier's knife.

He wanted to produce a nicer model for officers, and his breakthrough came in 1897 when he figured out a way to put blades on the back side of the knife and still use the same springs that worked for the front blades. He redesigned the handle, replacing the wood with red fiber, and added two more blades: a corkscrew and a small blade. And thus was born the officer's knife, which was patented on June 12, 1897.

This was the original Swiss Army knife.

Elsener's company, which would be renamed Victorinox in 1909, to honor Elsener's mother, Victoria, got its first competition in 1908 when a preacher named Theodore Wenger began selling pocketknives to the Swiss Army. Today those two companies are still the only official suppliers to the Swiss Army and the only ones allowed to put the Swiss white cross on their handles. Each sells twenty-five-thousand knives a year to the Swiss Army.

So what is a real Swiss Army knife? The basic Swiss Army knife—the one used by the army—has eleven functions: a nail file, two screwdrivers (standard and Phillips), a can opener, pliers, scissors, tweezers, a saw, an awl (reamer), and, oh yes, lest we forget, two knife blades.

Some of the fancier models may also have a bottle opener, a ballpoint pen, a compass, a corkscrew, a hook, a magnifier, an open-end wrench, a plastic toothpick, a ruler, a straight pin, or a wood chisel.

The Swiss Army knife does look impressive. So impressive, in fact that in 1960 the Russians displayed a Swiss Army knife they had found in Francis Gary Powers's U-2 plane, labeling it "CIA equipment."

Chapter 3

Paint and Decorating Department: Floor Coverings, Wall Coverings

RONNIE MATTHEWS CALLS IT The Loafers Club.

"Every morning we have six or eight regulars: John Russell, the county historian; Bob, he's a construction supervisor; Lum's a deputy; Randy works at the power company. A couple of others. They just drop in and hang out."

The members of the unofficial Loafers Club straggle in to Winfield Hardware. There's no "meeting time." On this morning John is here bright and early but the others are absent, running their businesses and affairs.

The Loafers know their way around Winfield Hardware. John eases over to the coffeepot, pours himself a cup, then settles into a solitary white plastic lawn chair at the intersection between Nuts and Bolts and Electrical Supplies.

"They help us a lot," Ronnie says of his Loafers. "They unload trucks, clean up."

It's true. When Randy wanders in after lunch, the first thing he does is empty the trash.

The hardware store today is what the feed store was a generation or two ago, back when there were farmers. It's a place where men get together. There are no hardware stores in the mall because that's not a man's place.

John, who is also referred to as "the Mayor of Skeeterville," says Winfield Hardware is the only gathering place left in Winfield. "They closed the restaurant."

The Loafers Club carries on a running conversation that members pick up on the fly. If you weren't around yesterday, you don't know that "the high cost of bull sperm" is a running topic today because a contractor came in from a local farm, "where they treat the bulls better'n they treat the boys who take care of them 'cause the bulls are more valuable."

As with most gathering spots the conversation frequently turns to politics. School consolidation is discussed; everyone seems against it. Then the hot topic arises. The fire bond.

This is a long-running topic. "The fire bond is twenty-five dollars for residential but businesses pay by the square foot," says Ron. "My assessment is five hundred dollars." No one thinks this is fair. And everyone supports Ronnie in his court battle against the bond.

But before the fire bond issues burns itself out—as old topics are wont to do—Lum arrives with new conversation fodder: last night's wreck out on the highway. Lum has special insight because of his law-enforcement position. "They couldn't tell if it was a man or a woman, that's how bad they were."

What is the ugliest color of paint?

That was an actual topic of conversation one day at my father's hardware store. My father wasn't part of the conversation. He just shook his head and smiled. The debaters were me, Lewis Flick, and Jim Farris. Jim and I were about the same age, young smart-alecky college boys. Flick was a frequent partner in our mischief. For us it was just something to break up the monotony. Flick always used to say he liked it best when the store was busy. "Time passes a lot quicker."

I liked it busy, too. It meant my father was making money, which meant I was benefiting—if that trickle-down voodoo economics really works.

But the hardware store isn't always busy. Rain will kill a good day. There aren't many folks doing fix-it jobs when it rains. Even indoor jobs get neglected on rainy days. Rainy days are just not conducive to do-it-yourselfing.

So when it rains, it bores. And the hardware store staff is looking for something—anything!—to do.

And on this particular day our thoughts turned to paint. Ugly paint.

And there are some seriously ugly paint colors. Can you imagine someone actually painting their bedroom Conch? So you always feel like you are at the beach, picking shells out of the bottoms of your feet.

We easily agreed on the worst name for a paint color: Raw Umber. Ugh. Burnt Sienna was second.

But the ugliest paint. Some of the lighter grays are pretty bad: They make a room look like it was formerly occupied by a four-pack-a-day Marlboro man. In the end it was a green that won our votes for ugliest paint color. The winner was Seafoam Green, which looked like someone puked in the Aquamarine paint.

They really haven't changed paint colors much in the thirty years since that debate. But they have changed the names. Seafoam Green now goes by names like Tattle Teal and Ardsley (Gray-Seal brand). If there's no way to describe Red to a blind man, I'd like to hear the explanation for Ardsley.

1 Gallon Dutch Standard Bone White Paint— $11.98

Paint was developed twenty-five thousand years ago by the caveman. It was the first home decorating product and Og used it to draw those primitive little stick figures on his cave wall. Actually, I prefer those primitive little stick figures to those prints of big-eyed children, but that's another story for another day.

The first cave paintings were found in caves in France and Spain and have little in common with the work of such later European painters as Seurat and Monet, although they do kind of resemble Picasso's work, if you look at them from the side and squint.

The stick figures were drawn with charcoal from the fire or juice from a berry or, yes, even blood. We won't speculate on whose blood, we'll just hope it was something without a face.

The manufacture of paint didn't evolve much until the Middle Ages, when artists began boiling resin and oil to create mixable paints. The first paint mill was built in Boston around 1700 by one Thomas Child. But he didn't mix paints. He just ground up pigment, which buyers would take home and mix with oil. D. P. Flinn patented a water-based paint in 1865. His paint also included potassium hydroxide, zinc oxide, resin, linseed oil, and milk. Milk! It didn't cover very well, but boy was it tasty. Actually, Flinn never got into manufacturing his invention.

So from the dawn of time it would be 24,900 years before it finally dawned on someone to actually sell the stuff already mixed.

That man was Henry Sherwin, whose name lives on in the paint brand he created.

But it took some convincing.

In 1870 when Sherwin told his partners in Sherwin, Dunham and Griswold, a paint component business, that he thought they should add a ready-to-use paint to their line, they took a vote. They voted two to one to dissolve the partnership.

Why would anyone buy ready-mixed paint when they could mix it themselves? they asked. Of such skepticism have been born many American industries, including fashion and fast food as well as paint.

So Sherwin sought out an old friend named Edward Williams and began the arduous task of developing this ready-mixed paint. It took ten years—the first nine and a half of which it was looking like his old partners might be right. But finally, in 1880, Sherwin-Williams developed paint pigments fine enough to remain suspended in an oil base, and thus was born the first commercial ready-to-use paint. Had Sherwin been a bit quicker in his development the entire first chapter of Mark Twain's *The Adventures of Tom Sawyer* might be different.

In the fifties and sixties, when I worked at my father's store, Dutch Boy was the best-known paint that no one ever used. Everyone knew Dutch Boy because of its indelible logo. Who didn't know that damned little Dutch Boy with his overalls and his Little Lord Fauntleroy hair?

The Dutch Boy logo was created in 1907 for National Lead Company, a consortium of twenty-five different manufacturers of white and red lead—the major components of paint at the time. While twenty-five companies under one banner was great for industry muscle it was hell on brand identification. It seems each of the twenty-five companies had a different brand. It was so confusing that the companies decided they needed a common logo for all of their products.

Advertising manager O. C. Harn remembered seeing a proposed advertisement drawn by artist Rudolph Yook, who used a Dutch boy in painter's overalls and wielding a paint brush. Yook took his idea from the fact that white lead was made by a process that had been standard in the Netherlands for centuries.

National Lead took Yook's sketches to portrait artist Lawrence Carmichael Earl at his Montclair, New Jersey, studio and commissioned a full-blown painting. Earl hired his next-door neighbor—a 9-year-old *Irish* lad named Michael Brady—to pose for the painting. Irish boy Brady didn't complain about portraying a Dutch boy and neither did his parents. After all Earl was paying him two dollars an hour to pose, the equivalent of supermodel pay today.

The Dutch Boy logo has undergone nine facelifts over the years, keeping his overalls, cap, and traditional Dutch hairstyle. The original Dutch Boy image was revived in 1987 and is the one you see on Dutch Boy paint cans today.

I don't know of any store in my hometown that sold Dutch Boy paint. Dutch Boy didn't market to the do-it-yourself crowd back then. It aimed at the construction industry. My father never carried Dutch Boy. He sold two brands: Kem-tone and Sherwin-Williams. By the time Dutch Boy added an exterior latex and got interested in the hardware store crowd, my father wasn't interested. In later years he added a third brand, Blue Ridge. It was a lot cheaper than the other two, but my father always swore it was just as good. My house is painted with it, and while it is fading some and chipping a bit, the paint job is fifteen years old.

Winfield Hardware doesn't sell Dutch Boy either. Ronnie used to carry it but now he sells the similarly named Dutch Standard paint. "I think this is better. I'll tell you how I picked it. My wife keeps up on the *Consumer Reports* magazine. They did a paint test and there were just a few companies that had the highest rating in interior and exterior. The biggest paint companies didn't make the list but this one did."

Few hardware stores carry Dutch Boy anymore. In 1984 Dutch Boy changed its marketing strategy to focus on the big home centers and discount stores. A few independent hardware stores carry it, but for the most part, if you want Dutch Boy, go to Wal-Mart or Home Depot.

Which paint should you use? What's the difference between the high-priced stuff and the low-end brand you've never heard of?

The industry has created several measures to determine the quality of a paint. There is "coverage," which measures a paint's hiding properties. It is determined by painting a black surface and a white surface. Unless you were a math major you probably don't care about the ratio of coverage delineation (and if you were a math major, you're probably not reading this book). Suffice to say that 0.98 is a top-grade paint.

Gloss is measured by reflecting light off a painted surface.

A paint's adhesive qualities are tested by sticking tape over a small crosshatch of dried paint and pulling. Top-grade paint doesn't come off.

A good paint can sit for six months without settling. In this test a rating of ten is tops.

To determine fire-retardant properties of a paint scientists burn it and see how much weight loss it suffers. If it loses more than 10 percent of its weight it can't be advertised as "fire retardant."

Ronnie Matthews has a simpler way to tell which is the best paint. "My experience with a gallon of paint is, if you want to know which is better paint, put 'em on a set of scales. You don't even have to open the can. The heavier the better. Water weighs eight pounds a gallon, anything else is product."

12-Ounce Spray Can Flat Black Rust-Oleum— $3.19

A paint that can cut through rust, coat the base surface, and even prevent future corrosion? Sounds fishy?

That's what folks who first heard about Captain Robert Fergusson's Anti-Rust Paint back in the twenties said. And they were right. It was fishy—the secret ingredient was fish oil!

Fergusson, an old salt who ran away from his Scotland home and went to sea at age twelve, noticed that his deck-polishing duties were much easier after a fish-oil spill. The fish oil stopped rust in its tracks and seemed to prevent further corrosion.

Even at twelve Fergusson saw he had stumbled onto something: He just wasn't sure what. And he knew that his fish-oil metal polish was no panacea. It had two major drawbacks: It took forever to dry and it smelled like fish!

So in 1919 when the now forty-two-year-old Fergusson was in charge of the World War I Victory Fleet in New Orleans, he decided to use his rusting fleet as a test laboratory. He cooked up fish oil resins in his ship's galley, combining them with other products until he hit on the right formula. After who knows how many attempts he created a fish-oil paint that stopped rust, dried quickly, and didn't smell like fish. So he founded the Anti-Rust Paint Company of New Orleans and began a quest to sell America on his product. He had much success—even in the face of competition from nine-hundred other American paint companies—until the Depression struck.

Fergusson died in 1940, before his antirust paint, now called Rust-Oleum, became a household word. It was left to his two sons, Robert and Donald, to guide the company.

Success was achieved at last in 1959 when the company began selling to the consumer market. My father's store was one of the first to stock Rust-Oleum. We never told people that the paint was a fish-oil formula. Because we didn't know that either.

Today's Rust-Oleum has an odor, but it's the lingering aroma of fresh paint. Nothing fishy about it anymore.

Ron had one bit of advice for Rust-Oleum users: "Don't put it on in hot weather. It won't dry. And don't put it on too thick. You're better off with a thin coat that you let dry. If you put it on all at one time, you'll have a terrible time getting it to dry. I just had an oil and gas company paint a gas line with it. They tried to paint it all at one time. Under normal conditions a coat two mils thick will dry in two hours. For every mil after that multiply by four. They put on three coats at once and it took several days to dry."

HARDWARE HA HA'S

Here's the joke of the day, or at least it seems like the joke of the day. The fellow in the Jay Dog Food ballcap and the paint overalls is the third customer today to tell it:

"You know the difference between a divorce in West Virginia and a tornado in Kentucky? No difference. Either way somebody loses a trailer!"

The hardware store, because of its relaxed atmosphere—contrast the low-pressure salesmanship of a hardware store to the high-pressure selling of an auto dealer—lends itself to a lot of joshing: joshing between customer and clerk, between clerk and customer, and between clerk and clerk.

Lots of jokes are swapped around the cash register.

Hardware humor is a joshing kind of humor. The jokes are directed at someone, usually an innocent.

Every industry has its own brand of humor. When I was a mathemetician (I don't let just anybody know about that period of my life), there was a formula going around that just cracked math guys up. It was this:

Integral cabin/dcabin =

Show that to a math guy and he will double over. That's the formula for a natural logarithm, commonly known as the natural log. So that answer is "natural log cabin."

When you get off the floor, I'll tell you about hardware humor.

Hardware guys like to josh about imaginary tools. Left-handed monkey wrenches. Left-handed screwdrivers. There is no such thing, of course. To make a right-handed screwdriver a left-handed screwdriver you just put it in your left hand. To make a right-handed monkey wrench a left-handed monkey wrench, you just turn it over and put it in your left hand.

The tool joke that'll get all but the most experienced hardware guy is this: Wheelbarrow seats.

Next time you're in a hardware store, ask the clerk if they carry wheelbarrow seats. If he scratches his head, you got him. If he says, "You mean the fitting on the axle?" he's trying to figure out a part that looks like a faucet seat. And you got him.

If he answers, "One passenger or two?" he got you.

FORMICA

You know when you go in a restaurant and order a Coke and the waitress asks, "Is Pepsi all right?" I hate that.

Not because I am some sort of Coke fanatic—I don't know that I could tell them apart in a blind taste test—but because it takes me back to the days working in my father's hardware store.

People would come in and ask if we sold Formica. And I would debate in my head: Do I tell them no, because we don't sell Formica, we sell one of Formica's competitors, Pionite? Do I tell them we sell Pionite, which is the same thing, wondering if they will believe it is? Or do I just tell them, Yes?

I always just told them Yes.

Some brand names are so well known that when people come in the hardware store they ask for a product by brand rather than by name. Formica is a prime example.

In this case, I guess the proper name would be countertopping. But no one ever goes in a hardware store and asks for countertopping. They just don't. Once in a blue moon you may get one of the hem-and-hawers who tells you a long tale, winding up with, "Anyway, I'm building some new counters and I need to put something on them. . . ."

More than eighty years after its invention, Formica is still the best-known name in countertopping, although there are other brands on the market, from Pionite to Micarta.

In 1913 Herbert Faber and Daniel O'Connor established a company to manufacture insulation for the booming electrical business. It was only a few years after Edison's electric light took off and the need for electrical insulation was there. Up to that time the mineral mica was favored for insulating. But Faber and O'Connor discovered they could achieve the same results with cheaper materials, layers of paper in a resin. They called their product Formica, because it was used "for mica." Get it?

In 1927 they tinkered with the product a bit, putting decorative paper in their laminate and mashing it on a flatbed press. The result was a countertop that was durable and decorative. When the post–World War II housing boom took off, Formica was on kitchen counters everywhere. It was *the* name in countertops.

In 1978 the FTC tried to revoke Formica's trademark, claiming it had become a generic term. The litigation lasted two years before Congress stepped in and told the FTC to back off.

Formica won the battle and I'm glad for them.

But I can tell you that from popular usage it's a generic.

Or maybe it's just that it's such a quality product that no one wants to settle for less.

ARMSTRONG LINOLEUM

There is an old joke that makes the rounds of state-houses shortly after a new governor—especially one of common, perhaps even redneck, origin—is elected. It has the new first lady heading over to the governor's mansion, to meet the outgoing first lady, to discuss decorating and to measure for lineoleum in the kitchen.

Linoleum is the floor covering of choice for the working class.

It was developed in the middle of the nineteenth century from flax and oil (the Latin words are linum and oleum, thus linoleum).

The big name in floor coverings is Armstrong and has been since 1860 when Thomas Armstrong bought a cork-cutting shop in Pittsburgh. He manufactured cork stoppers for bottles, at first cutting them by hand, then by machine. On the side he began selling cork sheets for floor covering. When linoleum was developed in the 1860s, he quickly sold off his cork business and switched over to making nothing but floor coverings. It was Armstrong who made floor covering affordable—and desirable—for the common man. He was the Henry

Ford of flooring, convincing housewives and farm wives alike that a linoleum floor was easier to clean than the old wood floors they were used to.

Winfield Hardware doesn't carry linoleum. Ronnie says, "I let Ken at Ken's Kitchens take care of that end of the hardware business for me."

Chapter 4

Lumber,
Miscellaneous

AT MY FATHER'S STORE, whenever someone backed up to the front door, you couldn't find a salesman. We scattered in all directions. It meant only one thing: concrete mix. My father carried concrete mix in two sizes: small hernia and large hernia. Actually it was forty-five-pound bags and ninety-pound bags. And we all hated to sell it because it meant you had to load it.

Ronnie Matthews laughs when I tell him that story. But it is a familiar laugh. He knows what I am talking about.

•   •   •

No sooner have we finished talking about this than a truckload of concrete mix arrives. If I'm lucky I might get to help unload it.

Normally Ron would scoot out on his hydraulic fork-lift and pick off the pallets in a heartbeat. But not today. The forklift is broken.

But Ron has an idea. "I'll send it on up to Leslie Lumber. He's a friend of mine. Let him unload it with his forklift."

Ron turns to the truck driver: "Do you mind taking it on up the road? A friend of mine's got a lumber yard and he'll unload it. Otherwise we got to unload it by hand. Is that okay?"

"That's okay by me." The trucker grins.

"I hate to do that but it's better than hand unloading."

"If you don't tell, I won't."

Deal.

60-Pound Bag Sakrete Concrete Mix—$9.98

Simply put, concrete is liquid stone.

The limy clay that was used to hold stone huts together—back in the days when Og was a common first name—was, strictly speaking, the first cement.

The Egyptians discovered that the chips from the blocks used to make the Great Pyramid could be burned and turned into mortar.

But it was left to the Romans to invent concrete—so I can thank Caesar for my hernia—and they originally made it from a cement of volcanic ash. Remember Pompeii? That was just a bounty for Julius Caementus the Cement Maker. The word cement —originally "caementum"—comes from the Latin word *caedere* meaning to cut down. It comes from the time when chipped stone was used to obtain cement material.

The Romans later developed a hardier concrete by mixing cement with water, lime, and rock. And concrete mix has been pretty much the same ever since. Concrete mix today comes in two styles: Sand mix is for smoothness, gravel mix is for jobs requiring a stronger concrete.

The Romans used cement in their hydraulic works, including the Great Aqueduct, which supplied Rome with drinking water for years.

The Pantheon, the Colosseum, and the Baths of Caracalla all were made of cement. But like barbershop harmonizing, the art of cement-making was lost during the Dark Ages. It was rediscovered in 1756 by one John Smeaton, who had been hired by the British Parliament to rebuild a burned lighthouse off the coast of Plymouth, England. After much experimentation, he found a material that would harden under water and still withstand the slashing ocean waves. He made his cement with some volcanic ash he had purchased at a local Plymouth warehouse, where it had been imported from Italy. He combined it with clay limestone and—Eureka!—cement. That lighthouse, the Eddystone Lighthouse, stood for 123 years and would have stood longer but was razed in a moment of historical-preservation weakness, only to be replaced by a taller tower.

Romans may have invented cement and Smeaton may have rediscovered the art, but it was left to a British bricklayer named Joseph Aspdin to perfect it. He shoveled up dust from local highways, where wagon wheels had crushed the limestone paving stones into dust. He was fined many times for stealing the public's dust, but he didn't give up. He kept at it, working on his formula for cement. In 1824 he turned his petty crime into gold when he received a patent for Portland Cement. "I take a specific quantity of limestone, *such as that generally used for making or repairing roads* [author's emphasis to make sure you note that Aspdin is confessing to a crime in a no-jury-would-convict-me kind of way] and I take it from the roads after it is reduced to a powder." He then mixed the dust with red clay, cooked it to a cinder, and pulverized that into a powder, which he mixed with water. The lime from the limestone reacted with the clay to form a gray pudding that hardened into concrete. Aspdin found his mixture surprisingly like the stone quarried on the Isle of Portland and thus dubbed it Portland Cement. Now you know what Portland Cement is.

The first U.S. patent for cement went in 1871 to David O. Saylor, who claimed his cement was superior to that of the British. His cement was named tops at the 1876 Centennial Exhibition in Philadelphia—they just don't have exhibitions like that anymore. Not even the county fair has a category for Best Cement.

Two years later U.S. engineers specified Saylor's cement for the Eads Jetties at the mouth of the Mississippi. Other American cement manufacturers were astonished that Saylor could make a Portland cement using homegrown ingredients, and within twenty years there were sixteen manufacturing plants turning out American Portland cement. By the turn of the century Portland cement use had passed natural cement use in this country.

The Industrial Revolution was a boom time for concrete-makers. Concrete was needed for everything from factory floors to sidewalks. Even Thomas Edison tried to get in on the great concrete boom; he reconfigured an ore-processing machine he had invented into a Portland cement mixer. To promote his product he designed the first all-concrete house, a low-priced domicile that could be built in a mere six hours! The wagon backed in and poured the house, including furniture, refrigerator, and piano. But the concrete piano never caught on and neither did Edison's invention.

It took one-hundred-thousand ancient Egyptians a lifetime to build the Great Pyramid. Today, with the miracle of cement, they could do it in a couple of years, three tops. Unless of course it was under a government contract. In which case it would take about the same length of time as the Egyptians and include cost overruns that won't even fit on this page.

In 1990 global production of Portland Cement was 1.3 billion tons, or about five-hundred pounds per person on planet Earth. How did you use your quarter-ton?

Since one cubic foot of concrete weighs 145 pounds, that figures out to about four cubic feet of concrete per person. That's about the size of a concrete piano. Where's Edison when you need him?

What should you look for in a cement mix? Cement, says Ronnie. "I sell Sakrete, which is government-approved. That means you can use it on a government project. A sixty-pound bag of Sakrete concrete mix has fourteen and a half pounds of cement. Some other brands will only put seven pounds in. That's okay for a post but make a pad with that and it's going to crumble on you. The most important thing about concrete mix is the amount of cement."

GROUT—$2.29

What do I know about grout? Aside from having the ugliest-sounding name of any product in the hardware store, not much. I always assumed it was just thin mortar, and it is. I know it rhymes with a couple of other ugly words: gout and lout.

And I know you use it to fill in the spaces between ceramic tiles.

But I don't know how to use those spacers they give

you with the grout. I know if you put them in sideways, you can grout over them. And if you stand them up, you have to pull them out. What's best?

My father always said to buy ceramic tile with the spacers built into the tile.

TRUE VALUE

You can go to a McDonald's in West Virginia or in Washington state and you know you are going to get the same thing: stainless-steel counters, clean restrooms, rock-hard plastic seats, and a menu of McSomething burgers.

But go to a True Value Hardware store in Washington and you will find it is completely different from one in West Virginia.

That's because McDonald's are franchises and True Value Hardwares aren't. True Value hardware stores are members. Call True Value Hardware a buying group and it might sound more familiar.

McDonald's may be locally owned but most everything the store does is dictated by the national organization. But nobody tells Ronnie Matthews that he has to sell four sizes of power drills and that he must call them Small, Regular, Large, and Super Size. His store isn't a franchise, but a member of a buying cooperative that purchases most of its inventory from a wholesaler that is owned jointly by all the hardware stores in the group.

There are four large dealer-owned hardware whole-salers: Cotter & Company with its True Value stores, Ace, American Hardware Supply, and HWI (Hardware Wholesale Inc.).

Winfield Hardware belongs to HWI, the smallest of the big four.

One in four hardware stores is a True Value store; one in five is an Ace Hardware. True Value and Ace are the McDonald's and Wendy's of hardware.

They are the ones that do the most national advertising. Here's a quick quiz to test the value of that advertising: Who does Ace Hardware commercials, John Madden or Pat Summerall?

You have a fifty-fifty shot.

Give? Madden does Ace; Summerall does True Value.

That doesn't prove that their advertising is worthless. You know both their names. That both use football announcers makes their advertising very similar.

True Value has at this writing 6,800 stores whose members buy 60 to 70 percent of their goods from the parent company, Cotter & Company of Chicago. Cotter is the largest hardware company in the world. It sold $2.4 billion worth of hardware in 1993.

Ace has 5,000 members and did $2.02 billion in sales in 1993.

Cotter started with 4 members in July 1947. By the end of the year, it had 25. There were 84 by the end of 1949 and 132 by the end of 1950. It was third among hardware coops in 1955 behind American and Our

Own. But in 1963 Cotter acquired Hibbard, Spencer, Bartlett & Co, and with it 400 dealers and the True Value trademark.

My father's hardware store was also a member of a buying cooperative. He affiliated with the Munford Do-It-Yourself Stores of Atlanta when he opened in 1955. His agreement was very loose: To use the Munford name—what value that was, I still don't know—he had to purchase at least one-hundred dollars a month from Munford, Inc.

My father dropped the Munford name—and was relieved of the buying requirement—in 1969, changing his store to The Do-It-Yourself Center. That year 24 percent of hardware stores were part of a buying group. By 1986 that had grown to 52 percent. Today it is approaching 60 percent. Group purchasing power is obviously more important today.

At Ace you have to buy a minimum of seventy-six-thousand dollars a year from the company. Other groups have different minumum purchase requirements. ServiStar requires forty-thousand dollars a year in warehouse orders. It charges a fee of twenty-five dollars a week for each week the dealer doesn't place an order of six-hundred dollars or more.

Ronnie acknowledges that the HWI name doesn't help him any at Winfield Hardware. But he says the company helps him in many other ways, from inventory control to price stickers. "It's a small price to pay for what I get."

To use the HWI name and to buy goods from HWI, Ronnie says he had to buy HWI stock. "You buy shares in the company when you first join. You have to keep a percentage of your yearly sales in stock, like 2 percent. Say you purchased two hundred thousand dollars from them, then you have to have four thousand dollars in stock. Now a percentage of what you sell you get back in rebate. But they hold a portion until you've built up enough stock. They're operating on your money . . . like everybody else."

Chapter 5
Electrical Supplies
Department:
Lightbulbs, Batteries,
Wire, Conduit

AN OLD FELLOW IN OVERALLS enters Winfield Hardware, his walk as baggy as his clothes. You don't see overalls in the hardware store the way you once did. Tee shirts and jeans are now the work uniform of choice.

"I need a plug for the end of my extension cord," he fairly shouts to clerk Kenny Smith.

"Male or female?" Kenny asks calmly.

It reminds me of the time my friend Larry Magnes spent half the day on his back, his arm twisted, his teeth gritted, wriggling a screw out of a rats-nest of U-traps and S-pipes and plastic tubing, all just to get to a tiny washer.

Sure enough, the washer was worn, and certainly the cause of his plumbing leak. He ran it down to our local hardware store.

As he later related it to me: "I handed it to the guy. I mean I was so proud of myself for getting it out without having to call a plumber. I don't know what I expected: a pat on the back, a little male bonding there with him asking me how long it took to get it out. The guy takes one look at it and says, 'Brass or copper?'"

Brass or copper?

Male or female?

Right-handed or left-handed?

These are the eternal hardware questions.

And no matter what your problem—electrical or plumbing, building or demolishing—the guys at the hardware store are one step ahead of you. They know the solution.

It was that way in the sixties, when I worked for my father at his little hardware store in east Tennessee. It was that way last week, when I took my own worn-out washer in to the hardware store to buy a replacement.

Fashions come and go. If you could recreate a women's dress shop from the fifties in a modern mall, people would laugh it out of business. But the modern hardware store is almost identical to the hardware store my father opened in 1955.

And the eternal hardware questions from then are the eternal hardware questions today: Brass or copper? Male or female? Right-handed or left-handed?

Hardware is forever.

4-PACK GE SOFT WHITE MISER LIGHTBULBS, 95 WATT—$2.99

The grade-school portrait of Thomas Edison's invention of the lightbulb is a simple one: boy genius (Edison was a mere thirty-one) retires to laboratory, draws a few sketches, fiddles around with a few wires, plugs in bulb, and presto! Electric light!

It wasn't that simple, of course. To begin with there was nothing for Edison to plug his bulb in to. There was no elaborate system of utility poles. Home electricity didn't exist. Part of the genius of inventing the electric light was inventing a generator to power it and devising a system to bring electricity into every home. Without the wall outlet, the electric light would be nothing more than an expensive table decoration.

And far from retiring to a sparsely furnished room to ponder the problem, Edison worked on it at his lab, a magnificent series of buildings in Menlo Park, New Jersey, a bucolic area twenty-five miles outside New York City. And he didn't skulk off in solitude; he had a veritable team of researchers, at times as many as thirty.

And it didn't happen overnight. It took almost two years.

Not to disparage the portrait of Thomas Edison as a genius. He was, both at science and at public relations. He had newspaper reporters eating from his hand, writing glowing—pun intended—portraits of his research. In March 1879 when Edison's research was at its low point, he convinced a *New York Herald* reporter that all was well. It wouldn't be any time before his new *platinum* lamp was ready for a public demonstration. As it turned out, platinum wasn't the material of choice for the lightbulb, but Edison didn't know that yet.

In an account typical of the breathless way Edison was covered, the *Herald* wrote: "The first practical illustration of Edison's light as a system has just been given. For the past two nights his entire laboratory and machine shop have been lighted up with the new light, and the result has been eminently satisfactory."

Edison told the paper there were only two steps left before the adoring public could have its electric light: "'The first is a standard lamp to be used and the second a better generator than the one now in operation.' Neither of these requirements is regarded by him as difficult of attainment." Let's see if we have this right: Edison has now perfected the electric light, except for the bulb and except for the method of providing electricity. Hmmm. Seems like he's got nothing, there, Mr. *New York Herald* reporter.

Edison actually entered the race to develop the electric light a bit late.

Scientists had been trying to invent an incandescent electric light since 1808 when Sir Humphry Davy had used a giant battery at London's Royal Society to prove that electricity could be used to produce light. There were patents issued for arc lights and incandescent lights in the 1840s. The problem wasn't getting an electric light to glow but keeping it glowing. The elements would glow for a time, then melt or oxidize.

Experimenters tried carbon and platinum. Carbon didn't melt but it did burn. Platinum was expensive and also required so much heat to produce incandescence that virtually every experiment ended with a puddle of molten platinum and darkness.

The Belgian inventor Jobard produced incandescent light by burning a carbon element in a vacuum as early as 1838. The Brit Sir William Grove did the same with platinum in air in 1840. Others did similar work—twenty-three in all, according to Arthur A. Bright's book *The Electric Lamp Industry.*

Of those twenty-three, eighteen used carbon as an element, fourteen used a vacuum.

Edison knew all this. He was very thorough when it came to researching the literature, at one time even assigning an assistant full time to the task. But Edison believed in his own genius, believed that he could prevail where many—many!—before him had failed.

Fresh from his success with the phonograph—the talking machine, which he had invented by accident—Edison set his sights on developing an incandescent light.

There was considerable interest in developing an electric light, but much of it was of the novelty kind. The world was not crying out from the darkness.

Fire had been the primary source of nonsunlight light from the Stone Age to the Gas Light Era: first were torches, then candles, followed by oil lamps and gas lights. The problem was that fire wasn't very good at illumination. And worse, it was only one false step from weak illumination to burning down the house.

Gas light was the greatest improvement over torches and by Edison's time most large cities had an intricate system of gas lights. But if you've ever tried to read by a gas light, you know it can't compete with an incandescent bulb.

There was a need, even if it wasn't a burning need. Or perhaps because it was a burning need, if you get what I mean.

And Edison took on the challenge.

Edison had two major advantages over his competitors. He was a genius, and that was important. But perhaps even more important, he had the deepest pockets, the richest funding of any of the inventors dabbling in electric light. Edison was financed by—are you ready for this?—the gas companies!

That's right, the folks who stood to lose the most if he did develop a cheap system of electric lighting. Talk about covering your bets.

Still it was no foregone conclusion that Edison would succeed. Not only did he have to invent the light, he had to devise it from cheap materials. It had to work and it had to work more cheaply than gas lights.

But he never questioned his ability to do this, positing in March 1879 that he could turn on electricity at a savings that would net him and his partners a tidy profit of almost three-quarters of a million dollars. A year!

Edison's research on the electric light began in earnest on August 27, 1878. He spent almost his entire first year fooling with a platinum filament, despite evidence from many researchers that platinum would melt after a short time.

In fact, on October 7, 1878, Edison even got a letter from another inventor, one Moses G. Farmer, who was also working on an incandescent light. Farmer had already abandoned platinum and was pursuing other materials for the light filament. He sent Edison a bar of iridium, suggesting it might work better than platinum. He also wrote that carbon "is the most promising— when sealed tightly from oxygen either in a vacuo or in nitrogen." Edison used the iridium bar and ignored the advice on carbon, effectively costing himself a year of research.

One of Edison's problems was that he wasn't familiar with mechanically produced electricity. All his work, on the telephone, telegraph, and phonograph, was with batteries. He had to learn about generators. And it was a long and costly lesson. Inventing this lightbulb was going to take longer than he had estimated.

While he was fending off an adoring public and press with one hand, Edison was stroking his investors with the other, trying to convince them that this was not a folly he was burying their money in. They had no reason to believe otherwise—he was after all Thomas Edison.

So in April 1879, Edison cranked out a series of calculations designed to show his moneymen that not only would the electric light be a brilliant invention, it would be a profitable one, too.

The customer was to get no savings in the equation. The home light bill would stay the same. The difference would all go to line the pockets of Edison and his partners. Did I mention that in addition to being a scientific genius and a public relations genius, he was also a business genius?

While the numbers sound great, they were fanciful figures, plucked from thin air, according to Robert Friedel and Paul Israel, authors of the definitive story of Edison's invention *Edison's Electric Light: Biography of an Invention*. But those numbers did keep the investors in the hunt.

After many false steps—all reported as giant advances by the press—Edison finally hit on the idea of the carbon filament. Duh. He got the idea for this filament after absentmindedly rolling a piece of compressed lampblack in his fingers until it became a slender piece of thread, just the size he was looking for as a filament!

For his end product Edison used carbonized cotton thread as a filament, clamped it to platinum wires and placed it in a glass bulb that was sealed at the neck. A vacuum pump evacuated the air. Lead-in wires hung from the bulb.

He ran the first test of this lamp on October 19, 1879: plugged it in. It burned for two days—forty hours—before burning out. Eureka, as they say.

Two months later Edison opened up his laboratory for a celebration of this new invention. The *New York Herald* described that New Year's Eve exhibition this way:

"Edison's laboratory was tonight thrown open to the general public for the inspection of his electric light. Extra trains were run from east and west notwithstanding the stormy weather, hundreds of persons availed themselves of the privilege. The laboratory was brilliantly illuminated with twenty five electric lamps, the office and counting room with eight and twenty others were distributed in the street leading to the depot in some of the adjoining houses." Edison put one bulb under water for four hours with no perceptible effect. Another he turned on and off repeatedly and rapidly, simulating thirty years of turning on and off, with no problem.

The science part was over; the business part now began. The Edison General Electric Company was organized by one of Edison's business partners, Henry Villard. In 1892 General Electric was formed. It was a patent pool bringing together the Edison folks, who had the incandescent lightbulb patents, with their rivals from the Thompson-Houston Company, which had the patents to the alternating-current transformer.

Before the turn of the century General Electric was using the initials GE in a swirling circle logo, the GE trademark that is now synonymous with the lightbulb. Company records trace the logo to a sales committee meeting of July 1, 1899, but no one knows who actually created it.

The lightbulbs I hold in my hand today are changed from Edison's original invention. For one thing modern lightbulbs use tungsten filaments, not carbon ones, because tungsten can withstand temperatures up to forty-five-hundred degrees Fahrenheit. And the vacuum inside the bulb has been replaced by argon and nitrogen gas. But the base is still known as the Edison screw base.

Despite these changes the lightbulb is very much Edison's child. And a century later it is still perhaps the most inefficient everyday bit of hardware: 95 percent of the electricity that goes to a lightbulb is converted to heat instead of light. But Edison didn't invent the lightbulb for efficiency. Fluorescent bulbs are more efficient and last longer but, as anyone will tell you, they hurt the eyes. Edison's bulb was invented to produce artificial light as close as possible to that from the sun. And that it does.

The importance of the invention of the lightbulb goes way beyond just the ability to read John Grisham novels into the wee hours. In inventing the electric light Thomas Edison effectively created the electric power industry, which provides the power and impetus for all the wondrous inventions of the twentieth century: television, radio, computers. If not for Edison, there would be no Oprah.

Ironically, the day generally given for Edison's invention of the electric lightbulb—October 21, 1879—is actually the day the first electric lightbulb burned out.

12-INCH GE FLUORESCENT BULB—$2.98

Edison's incandescent light reigned for half a century, until GE scientist Dr. Arthur Compton created a fluorescent light in 1934. The fluorescent bulb was cheaper to operate and cooler to the touch but its light was harsher than incandescent light, so it didn't immediately run Edison's creation out of the marketplace.

In fact, today fluorescent and incandescent light coexist—peacefully—side by side.

The French had been working on a fluorescent light since the 1850s. Physicist Antoine-Henri Becquerel, the same guy who discovered that uranium was radioactive, coated the inside of a glass tube with phosphor and watched that baby glow.

There is no chemical "fluoro"—the name comes from the verb "fluoresce," which is what some elements do when they give off light as they absorb radiation.

The fluorescent light was introduced at the 1939 World's Fair in New York City and by the time my father opened his store in 1955, fluorescent and incandescent bulbs were selling about equally. This wasn't because the fluorescent bulb was moving into the home but because businesses liked the lower costs of fluorescent lighting.

Next time you're in a store, look up. Odds are you'll see a fluorescent light.

TAKING STOCK

The biggest difference between Winfield Hardware and my father's store, the major advance of the last twenty years, is in ordering stock. Ronnie has a little hand-held computer, a Texlon, he calls it, that he uses to order. My father would wander around his store with what he called his little Want Book, writing down items that were low or that he was out of. Ronnie wanders around with his Texlon, punching in a six-digit product code for items he needs. Then he adds the number he wants to order and when the computer's memory is filled up, he sends his order electronically over the phone to his co-operative buying group, HWI.

He knows the product's code because it's on a sticker on the bin.

For instance, an electrical box has this sticker: "507614 box, 1/2 gm k 34 6 11/4."

"507614" is the product catalog number.

"box, 1/2 gm" means it is a gem box, a common electric box that measures two inches by three inches by two and one half inches deep.

"k" means it's a popular item. "If you see the 'k' next to an item in the catalog, it gives you an idea if you want to try carrying it."

"'6 11/4" means "I last ordered six of them on 11/4."

The "34" is the profit margin, meaning Ronnie is making a 34 percent profit, about average for his store, he says.

Orders arrive in large plastic tote boxes, about the size of a mover's box, with preprinted price stickers.

When I was my father's stock boy, I would spend half a day opening boxes, matching items to the invoice, then pricing the items. My father used a 50 percent markup, which meant if his price on the invoice was $1.00, he would price it to sell at $1.50. Actually he liked the -9 system, so I would price it at $1.49. Then I had to put the stock out on the shelves. Ronnie used the old stocking system and says his present high-tech inventory system cuts stocking time in half.

BILL SMITH

My father has been dead ten years, his store out of business for fifteen, and I still have Summers Hardware ball-point pens—twenty-one at last count. Summers Hardware was his equivalent of HWI, Winfield Hardware's primary wholesaler. My father bought from Munford and Belknap Hardware in Louisville and Allied in Chattanooga but his primary supplier, the entire time he was in business, was Summers Hardware, twenty miles away in Johnson City, Tennessee.

You may have heard of Johnson City: It's the home of East Tennessee State University. When I was growing up, people were always saying, "Johnson City's like Little Chicago." You get the idea. It was a bit more wide open than Kingsport. For instance, in Johnson City, you could buy beer! You could in Kingsport, too, but you had to know somebody.

My father's connection to Summers Hardware was a big friendly guy as common as his name: Bill Smith. Twice a week, on Monday and Thursday, he would lumber into the store carrying what looked like a bowling ball case but was in fact his catalog. He would spring for Pepsis all around, then take his catalog back to the office, where he would sit, nursing that Pepsi while he wrote out the store's order.

He had a meticulous script—I can still see it today, a result of my checking the delivery against the invoice twice a week during my youth. It usually took him about an hour; then he lumbered out and the next afternoon the Summers Hardware truck would show up at the back door, ready to be unloaded. Even then truck drivers would only tailgate the load. I had to drag the boxes off and stack them, hoping like hell that the breakable stuff didn't get crushed under the heavy stuff.

Summers Hardware was an old company by the fifties. It was founded in 1893 as Summers Barton Hardware Company, a retail hardware store. In 1910 the owners divided the retail and wholesale divisions and sold off the retail.

The company's best selling item in the early years was railroad ties; this was when the Clinchfield Railroad was being built.

Once the railroad was finished, the Depression hit and hit hard. Summers, always easy with its accounts, nearly went under. The company reorganized in 1936 after credit losses from the Depression. This was when F. L. Wallace became associated with the firm, according to a company history. I think that means he bailed them out. His son F. L. Wallace, Jr., is president today. The wholesaler stocks thirty thousand items in a two-hundred-thousand-square-foot warehouse. It employs twenty-two salesmen to work its distribution territory in Tennessee, Virginia, Kentucky, and North Carolina.

Bill Smith is no longer there. A bad hip and deteriorating vision forced him to retire long before my father closed his store. He died the same year as my father.

I'm just glad I stocked up on all those old Summers Hardware promotion pens—they were nice Paper Mates. I haven't bought a ballpoint pen in my entire life. And I'm a writer.

DURACELL 9-VOLT BATTERY—$2.19

For me, the battery ranks right up there with the television set and the flushing toilet as the most magical of inventions. The battery is a walking power plant! Many of them are no bigger than your thumb: Some of them are the size of an aspirin. Imagine all the things the battery has made possible: portable drills and vacuums, the camcorder, the flashlight, the Walkman.

The first battery was made almost two centuries ago, in 1800, by the Italian physicist Alessandro Volta. Instead of naming the battery after him, science has honored him instead by giving a unit of electric measurement, the volt, his name. Which brings up the question—probably already asked by Alessandro—of why science didn't call the unit named after him the "volta." I don't know: Sounds too much like a river? Anyway that's someone else's book. But I imagine it could make a pretty funny Far Side cartoon.

Volta created the battery by alternating silver and zinc discs with leather soaked in salt. He attached strips of metal at each end and he connected the strips to cups of mercury. Then when he stuck his fingers in each cup, he got a shock. The more layers of discs he piled up, the stronger the jolt. Yes, it seems a little silly, except perhaps in an S&M parlor. But to create an electric charge from such simple ingredients was quite an achievement for 1800. Remember, Ben Franklin risked electrocution a few years earlier just to see if those lightning bolts really were electrical as he suspected. A little tingle in the fingers was nothing compared to the pop ol' Ben got.

Word of Volta's experiment traveled slowly. It would be thirteen years before the British scientist Sir Humphry Davy would try to replicate it. He did, using two thousand discs instead of a handful. His "voltaic pile" (Volta's name for the battery) produced a strong enough charge to remove sodium and potassium from compounds.

The French, for reasons known only to the French, took to this battery resarch. In 1859 Frenchman Gaston Planta made a lead-acid battery that could give a real jolt. During the next decade another Frenchman, Georges Leclanche, invented the dry cell battery. In fact it was Leclanche's dry cell that powered Alexander Graham Bell's first telephone. Even today cordless and cellular phones are powered by battery.

So the battery is really just a chemistry experiment that worked.

We are a nation of battery-using fools. We use twenty-seven batteries a year *each* in this country. I'll bet you can't look around the room you are currently in and not see something that is battery-powered. (Unless you are in the smallest room in the house.)

The most popular battery in use today is the alkaline battery, so called because it uses alkaline as an electrolyte, and not—as is believed by some hard-core baseball fans—because its performance is as steady and consistent as that of former Detroit Tiger outfielder Al Kaline. But here is where the alkaline bettery resembles the other Al Kaline. It loses its power gradually, about 4 percent a year on the shelf. The ballplayer Al Kaline was like that.

It's probably just as well that old Alessandro Volta got

a unit of electrical measurement named after him instead of the battery. How many people would have enough nerve to go into the store twenty-seven times a year and ask for a voltaic pile? Sounds too much like a hemorrhoid cream to me.

Chapter 6
Plumbing
Department

RANDY, A CHARTER MEMBER of Ronnie's Loafers Club, spends a couple of hours a day, most days, at Winfield Hardware, helping out, picking up. Never getting paid. "I just like being around hardware stores," he says. Lots of men do.

This soft spot for all things hardware didn't arise with comedian Tim Allen and his comedy routines that inspired the hit TV series *Home Improvement*. Fred C. Kelly professed his love for hardware in a 1958 issue of *The Rotarian*, proclaiming, "Perhaps no other kind of store stirs so many human cravings."

Changing Times in 1955 said, "The hardware store is

to the average man what the dress or hat shop is to a woman."

O-RING— 10 CENTS

Many of the names of hardware-store items come from what the items look like.

The bone wrench looks like a small bone.

The C-clamp is shaped like a C.

The U-Bolt is shaped like a U.

Likewise for an O-Ring, an S-Trap and a J-Bend.

The Tee and the Y Branch are pieces of pipe fitting that look like those letters of the alphabet.

Of course sometimes this method of naming can become nonsensical, giving us the Four-Way Tee, an alphabetical and geometric impossibility but a plumbing item, nonetheless.

Whoever named these products, way back in hardware antiquity, was especially fond of names with alphabet or animal connotations.

There are sawhorses, which look like horses, if you don't look too long or too hard. There's the crowfoot wrench, the gooseneck bar, the bullnose plane, the butterfly hinge, the cat's paw nail puller, clamshell moulding, duckbill snips, hawk's bill snips, and the plumber's snake, all of which have a resemblance to the animal they are named for. Even the monkey wrench looks like a monkey, although, as we have seen, it wasn't named for its jungle counterpart.

And some hardware items have downright lascivious names. Would you send your daughter into the hardware store to pick up a ballcock? Would you tell your little boy to stop on the way home from school and get you a two-inch nipple? Among the daring hardware names are the bastard-cut file (which is between a rough file and a fine file and has been called that at least since 1677), the reamer (ouch!), and the deep throat socket wrench. And don't even mention the electrical section where you must differentiate between a male plug and a female plug (yes, the difference has sexual overtones).

The most lascivious name in the hardware store? My choice is in the plumbing department: the eccentric nipple extractor. I don't even want to know what it does.

DANCO TOILET TANK LEVER — $3.69

Television is a marvel. Satellite TV is a miracle.

I don't understand how anyone could have envisioned the radio or the telephone or the record player before they existed.

In other words, modern times amaze me.

But the most amazing modern invention doesn't have anything to do with Roseanne's humor or Madonna's vocal cords. It is the flushing toilet. Imagine! It takes the things we don't want and it exorcises them from our houses.

It makes winters bearable.

And it does it all without electricity or even a battery.

You don't have to plug the toilet in.

And it was invented by a man with the unlikely name of Crapper. Actually it may be the likeliest of names.

Thomas Crapper was a Brit, and a hard-working one at that: born in Yorkshire, apprenticed to a Chelsea plumber at age eleven.

He wasn't even a teenager and he was working sixty-four-hour weeks. Tell that to McDonald's personnel director.

Crapper was fixing pipes in the same neighborhood as the painter Whistler and the poets Swinburne and Rossetti. Apparently they paid in cash, not verse, because at age twenty-four he opened his own shop, Thomas Crapper & Co., Sanitary Appliances.

It was 1861, a great time for makers of sanitary appliances. London had just built its first two main sewers. Over the next half-decade those pipes would be extended to a network of eighty-three miles.

Then in 1872 Parliament passed the Metropolis Water Act, aimed at straightening out Britain's confusing water situation: There were no fewer than eight separate water companies serving London alone, each with its own rules and regulations. The main thrust of the law was to prevent an alarming waste of water.

Toilets at the time were nothing more than a water pipe with a plug. Some lard-ass Londoners were too lazy to replace the plug after each poop, thereby allowing the water to run continuously. In their defense, some of these folks might simply have had bad valves. Few plugs in use at the time stayed watertight for long.

But Parliament, envisioning a dried-up land devoured by famine, pestilence, and poop, set out to do something about the sanitation problem.

Sanitation *was* a significant problem at the time. There is the story—perhaps apocryphal—of Queen Victoria being escorted across the Cam River bridge by a Dr. Whewell, the master at Trinity College. Spotting debris in the river below, she inquired, "What are all those pieces of paper floating down the river?" To which the quick-witted Whewell—he didn't get to be master for nothing—replied, "Those, Your Majesty, are notices that bathing is forbidden."

Thomas Crapper got in on the ground floor of the plumbing boom. England needed a functioning flush toilet.

Crapper's biographer Wallace Reyburn admits in *Flushed with Pride: The Story of Thomas Crapper* that our hero was not alone in working on the flushing toilet. He built on others' work and perfected the flushing toilet. "More than a few plumbers took up the challenge and just as a hundred years previously the work of James Watt and others had culminated in his producing the first efffective modern steam engine, so it was that there came into being 'Crapper's Valveless Waste Preventer. One Moveable Part only. Certain Flush with Easy Pull. Will Flush When Only Two-thirds Full.'" (Don't even think about what that "two-thirds full" means.)

Thankfully Crapper didn't try to trademark that name. What he did was patent his invention, British Patent No. 4,990, awarded in 1884.

Crapper's device was strikingly similar to the modern flushing toilet; the only difference was he used a pull chain instead of a handle.

Now the flushing toilet didn't happen overnight. Crapper had worked for years perfecting the device. In his workshop he had five toilet models for his experiments. Gentle readers will be pleased to know that he didn't practice with the real thing, employing instead apples, sponges, cotton waste, grease, and "air vessels"—essentially wadded-up pieces of paper.

There is a plumbing industry story—apparently true—that has Crapper once snatching an apprentice's cap as a "test soil." The eureka cry—the plumbing history equivalent of "Watson, Come here!"—was "It works!"

In recognition of his achievement Crapper was later appointed Royal Sanitary Engineer to His Royal Majesty King Edward VII.

Crapper's toilet—which he always referred to as a W.C., for water cistern, or water closet—took off. Soon designers got in on the act, creating fancier and fancier models. The first thronelike toilet—the first one to look like a modern toilet—was the Unitas, introduced to the world in 1885 by the British pottery firm of Twyford. It was touted as "The Perfection of Cleanliness . . . no Wood Fittings are required except a hinged seat which being raised, free access can be had to all parts of the Basin and Trap, so that everything about the Closet can be easily kept clean."

Crapper didn't quit with the flushing toilet. He invented a slew of other contraptions, including the "Seat Action Automatic Flush," which flushed itself after the master was finished, and the "Self-Rising Closet Seat," which popped back up after the master dethroned. Neither was a winner and both were eventually discontinued.

He kept on building toilets until his death in 1910, marketing them under such inspired names as the Cascade, the Niagara, the Rapido, and the Deluge.

Crapper, as a euphemism for toilet, is an American invention. Soldiers stationed in Britain during World War I noted the many toilets had the name "T. Crapper, Chelsea" imprinted on them and began referring to the john as the crapper. They carried the term back home, and by 1930 the *Dictionary of American Slang* reported it in common usage.

Crapper's name has been immortalized by Americans.

Hardly a day goes by that I don't think of Mr. Crapper. Every time I sit down with my magazine.

BALLCOCK FILLER TUBE—$2.29

The ballcock actually predates the flushing toilet. It was mentioned as early as 1850 when *Knight's Practical Dictionary of Mechanics* noted that a House service pipe was "provided with a ball-cock." The name has no sexual connotation, although it sure looks like it should.

"Ball" because it is a ball. "Cock" because that's what it does: sit cocked and ready to act.

The Endless Flush

I admit I am not the world's greatest "handyman." In fact, I usually deem it a success if I can take a broken appliance apart and put it back together again and it is no worse than it was before.

But the one area where I am totally inept is plumbing. It must be genetic. My father had the same problem with things plumbed.

So because of this awful character deficiency, when something in the bathroom breaks, tears, stops, falls apart, deteriorates, or otherwise ceases to work in its normal fashion, I insist on trying to fix it.

It happened on a recent Sunday. Of course. Things always break on Sunday. Why would my plumbing decide to operate continuously when the plumber is in his shop? No, it was a Sunday.

It all slipped up on me in the wee, small hours of the morning. Sometime between rise-time and shine-time, our commode decided to begin a cycle of continuous, self-originated flushing. After a period of about two hours, during which time my fix-it efforts were confined largely to walking into the bathroom every so often to see if the commode had healed itself, I determined that I would have to act.

So I removed the back lid and watched the inner

workings as they continued on their cycle of continuous flushing. The movement reminded me of a liquid clock.

After debating the philosophical implications of consuming five gallons of water to plunge away forever one ounce of waste, I slowly immersed my hand into the water. It was cold.

Only now what do I do? I jiggled something that looked like it should be jiggled. Nothing. I jogged something that looked like it should be jogged. Nothing. I firmly grasped a dingly thing and pulled up. And all the water went out.

It was then that the lightbulb clicked on. In one swell swoop I solved the problem. I called my uncle. The one who can fix plumbing. He's on my mother's side.

He doesn't live right next door, but I didn't mind the wait. By the time he got to my house, I was kind of enjoying watching the "Endless Flush." It was much better than *The Facts of Life*" and almost as good as *Family Matters*.

He rolled up his sleeve, plunged in his hand, jiggled the jiggle, jogged the jog, pulled up the dingly thing and said:

"You're gonna have to have a new one of these," pointing to the plastic lopsided water tower with the rubber hose coming out of its bottom.

Thank goodness for the giant home improvement center, which is open twenty-four hours a day, seven days a week, or any time anyone reaches into his or her billfold. It was there that Uncle and I purchased my

$3.97 guaranteed, genuine, plasticlike, lopsided water tower.

Meanwhile, back at the house, we determined that the water would have to be turned off before beginning the repair job. No valve on the commode. None in the basement. None on the side of the house. Finally we decided to turn off the main valve — the one under the giant metal footprint with "Water" imprinted on it and that is conveniently located so that passing cars have to swerve to miss you. The Water Company has placed a valve there much like the childproof caps that come on medicine: Not only does it prevent children from opening it, it also prevents anyone with strength less than Alex Karras's from getting in.

After two broken wrenches and a lot of hammering, we finally got the water turned off. The water tower was also designed to prevent children from getting it off. Thirty minutes of groaning later, the old was off, the new was on, and the only problem was getting the water back on.

It wasn't easy but we did it (we meaning Uncle). It was while admiring our success that Uncle noticed a tiny trickle of water emerging from underneath the commode. We'd solved the problem of the Endless Flush, but in the meantime, we had created a leak of our own. Back to the water main again.

It was then that Uncle informed me that he had to go. Actually, he deserved to go—he was hot and sweaty and I wasn't paying him anything.

So there I sat. With dirty hands, dirty body, a leaky commode, and no water.

After much serious discussion with myself about the advisability of moving to another place and letting the next inhabitant worry about the Endless Flush, I gathered myself together and returned to the bathroom, wrench in hand. I took the valve off, inserted a washer, and tightened it up again. I went back outside and after much struggle I heard the welcome gush of water through the pipes. I raced back inside to inspect my handiwork. Slowly I rotated my fingers around the mysterious joint. No water. I dried it off with a towel and checked it again. Dry. Still dry. I'd done it. I'd stopped the leak.

Only. Only what's that sound. Is it? It was. The Return of the Endless Flush.

DELTA CHROME KITCHEN SINGLE-HANDLED FAUCET SET—$64.98

Before Alex Manoogian all faucets were like the one in your grandmother's house: The handle with the H was for hot, the one with C for cold (unless Grandpa had been in the sauce when he installed the set), and with a little tinkering you could get it to dispense the proper mix of hot and cold water through the spigot.

In 1954 Manoogian, an engineer and metal worker, won a small contract to manufacture a new single-handled faucet. This new design, developed by the

Phelps Company of Compton, California, was dubbed the "one-armed bandit" by plumbers because it robbed homeowners of their money. In short, it didn't work.

But Manoogian redesigned the faucet, bought a license from the original patentholders, the Phelps family, and began marketing his new Delta faucet.

Housewives liked the new design. They could flip the handle to a certain predetermined angle and count on the correct water temperature for dishes. By 1958 Delta faucets were a million-dollar business—this at a time when a million dollars was very nearly worth a million dollars. Today Delta sells more than a million dollars in faucets over a weekend.

Ronnie sells Delta and recommends it. But he says the most important thing when you go in to buy plumbing supplies is: "Be sure when you buy one that the availability of parts is there. Plumbing is something you're going to have to work on. Chain stores sell one brand today and a year from now they don't have parts. Buy a name brand."

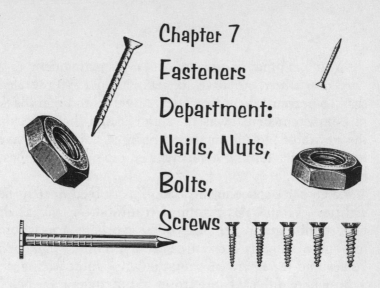

Chapter 7
Fasteners Department: Nails, Nuts, Bolts, Screws

JOHN GIBSON HAS BEEN WORKING at Winfield Hardware for seventeen years. Kenny Garner has been here three years. Ronnie's son and his nephew fill in the rest of the time. That means Winfield Hardware hasn't had to hire and train a new employee in years. I kid Ronnie that he doesn't know what personnel problems are. He agrees.

Whenever two small businessmen get together, talk inevitably turns to one topic—and it's not the availability of capital for expansion or the effect of a national health-care system on small-business insurance. No, it's about personnel: getting it, keeping it, and getting rid of it when it doesn't work out.

"You can't find good help" is a universal lament.

A *Hardware Age* survey of retailers in 1990 revealed that 16 percent of hardware-store owners thought "lack of competent help" was the number-one threat facing the health of their business; 64 percent claimed to have had difficulty finding competent employees in the past five years.

Retail sales space in this country doubled during the eighties. Retail sales positions traditionally pay at or near minimum wage. But young workers, for whom minimum wage is attractive, are a declining category. Fewer and fewer are entering the work force each year.

So where are hardware stores going to get their help?

The big chain home centers have been known to steal experienced hardware-store clerks by paying them two and three dollars an hour more than the grandpa-and-grandma stores.

That leaves small businesses on the outside looking in.

I have a friend who owns a small maid service. She claims to have hit on a simple solution. "I hire everyone who applies," she says. "Half of those never show up. And the half that does show, usually washes out in three days." She has a standing classified in the local Sunday paper.

Getting good help isn't a new problem. I can remember my father lamenting, "I hire the handicapped."

He didn't have hiring problems when he first opened his hardware store. He and his partner, Mr. Meade, ran the store themselves. One went to lunch, the other took over all the duties.

Their first employee was a gangly man with an enlarged Adam's apple and a perpetual five-o'clock shadow.

His name was Pat Davis, and he may have been thin but he was strong. I remember seeing him hoist a ninety-pound bag of cement mix over one shoulder, then stoop down and flip a second ninety-pound bag over the other shoulder. And not even breathe heavy.

He seemed like a grown man to me; he certainly had a man's beard. He was married and serious-minded. But when I was older I learned he was only twenty-one when he was working for my father.

I don't know how long Pat Davis worked for Meade & Staten, Inc. A year, two years? Those store records were discarded long ago. I remember he was at the little store on West Sullivan and he moved with them to the bigger store on West Sullivan. But he was gone by the time I was the stock boy.

He left for a construction job. I couldn't understand why he would leave a good job, where he got to wear a tie and work in the air-conditioned comfort of a store, for a sweaty, back-breaking construction job. That's when my father explained the facts of retail life to me: "I couldn't pay him enough."

Hardware is not the road to riches. It put me through college, but it never bought me a Mercedes. As a matter of fact I drove a 1955 Chevy, back when it wasn't a classic but just an old car. According to a 1988 *Hardware Age* survey 84 percent of all hardware-store owners make less than $40,000 a year. A quarter make less than $20,000.

And sales clerk at a hardware store is also no ticket to ride. That same survey revealed that 87 percent of all hardware-store clerks make less than $15,000 a year! Only 1 percent make more than $26,000 for schlepping hardware. The median salary for a clerk is just $10,800. For an owner it's only $28,000. On the other hand, hardware is the safest bet in the entrepreneurial field. Fewer new hardware stores fail than any other business.

So why do retired guys and young kids work at hardware stores? Two big benefits: paid vacations and—best of all—discounts on the merchandise. Ninety-eight percent of hardware stores give their employees a break on their tool purchases.

My father was joking when he said he hired the handicapped, but at one time it seemed that statement had been prophetic: He had a crippled salesman, an epileptic salesman, and a retired baseball player, who would have qualified as a lazy salesman.

Ronnie allows as how some hardware stores have success hiring retired fellows. "They work cheap and they show up on time. And they know hardware." But most stores still have to fill in from the under-twenty-five labor pool, a singularly unreliable and unmotivated group.

And there are problems with retired workers: They

aren't getting better every day. They are getting more feeble, more error-prone. One retired fellow worked for my father for twenty years—until my father closed his store—and never learned how to work the cash register. My father used to say he could count on Dewey for at least one hundred-dollar over-ring a week.

But my maid-service friend can top any hiring horror story. "One job applicant said he was a good worker and that he'd be an even better one when he finished his surgery. I figured he was getting a hernia repaired or something like that but, no, that wasn't it. He said he was having a sex change operation and he figured when he finally became a woman he would be a lot better housekeeper!"

Ronnie's hiring secret at Winfield Hardware? He doesn't have one. "John had been laid off at Southern Supply in Nitro. He didn't like unemployment so he came to me. He said, 'Whatever you'll pay me, I'll work for it.' He's been here ever since." Seventeen years! There are hardware-store owners who would kill for an employee like that.

BOX OF 9 NUMBER 6 1½-INCH FLAT-HEAD SLOTTED WOOD SCREWS—$1.09

The invention of the screw is generally credited to the Greek mathemetician Archimedes but he didn't mean for it to be used as a fastener. His screw was used to draw water from ships and keep them from sinking. He came up with his design during the third century B.C. and it was really just a worm and gear assembly tilted at about a forty-five-degree angle. Turn the crank and water is forced up the screw wall until it empties out at the top. It worked.

Another of his inventions—a war engine—prolonged the Roman siege of Syracuse by three years. For his cleverness Archimedes was lanced to death by a Roman foot soldier, who had been specifically ordered not to kill him. (Another employee horror story there. . . .) The Romans had plans for this genius.

And Archimedes *was* a genius. He considered his greatest discovery to have been a mathematical formula: "The volume of a sphere is two-thirds that of a cylinder."

I have my own favorite Archimedes discovery: to allay the suspicions of King Hiero II, who was just sure that the royal crown wasn't pure gold, Archimedes came up with the theory of density—a body displaces a body of water equal to its own bulk. The crown was impure, the goldsmith was executed, and this is where my favorite discovery comes. Racing home to explain his discovery of density, Archimedes repeatedly shouted "I have found it! I have found it!" except he didn't speak English, so he shouted it in Greek: "Eureka! Eureka!" Inventors ever since have used the term "Eureka" to signify a noteworthy discovery. Thanks, Archimedes.

Back to the screw . . . the first practical use was in

wine presses in the first century B.C. Thanks again, Archimedes.

It wasn't until the fifteenth century that metal screws and nuts appeared as fasteners. But these screws didn't have slotted heads. The heads were square or hexagonal and were turned with a wrench. The first slotted screws were used to make armor in the sixteenth century.

The screwdriver is a descendant of the flat-headed bit used in the carpenter's brace in the middle of the eighteenth century. The first screwdrivers were flat their entire length. Today's screwdrivers are stronger because they have a round shaft flattened at the end.

The modern screwdriver is the most ubiquitous of tools because it is cheap and because you always need several sizes and kinds on hand.

Winfield Hardware sells screws by the screw, but it also sells them in those little boxes, you know, with some unfathomable number of screws, like seven, in a pack. Ronnie says some people like to buy them in a box for convenience.

Why do some plastic boxes of screws have seven screws, while others have eleven and others fifteen? That dates back to the early days of self-service. The first prepacked boxes of screws were introduced at the Seventh National Hardware Show in 1952 by Eagle Lock of Terryville, Connecticut.

In describing Eagle Lock's display *Business Week* said, "Supermarket techniques are capturing the staid old hardware store."

Hardware stores were fighting back against the housewares sections of the supermarkets by using the competitor's own weapons: mass display, self-service racks, and packages with descriptive labels.

Eagle Lock displayed its Self Service Screw Merchandizer, the public unveiling of what became today's dreaded packages of screws. The plastic boxes came in sixteen sizes. The number of screws in each package varied so the merchant could charge the same for each box.

Business Week quoted an unidentified New Jersey hardware-store owner who expressed his pleasure with the new marketing technique. "I don't give a hoot if the profit margin on screws is reduced—it will be worth it to save the time fishing around in drawers for a handful."

So now you know how the screw manufacturers decide that you need seven screws. It works out that way so the package can cost the same as other packages of screws.

Thanks, Eagle Lock.

FLICK

Of the hundred or so employees who cycled through my father's hardware store in the thirty-odd years he was open, my favorite was Flick.

Lewis "Lefty" Flick couldn't seem to last more than two years at a stretch with my father. Then he'd take an insurance job for a while. "I like the hours better," he'd wink. "Get more fishing done." His long-suffering wife just kept on plugging away at her sales job at Penney's, supporting the family, while Lefty dabbled.

Lefty's wanderlust was understandable, once I knew his story. Of course it was years before I knew his story. Lefty was the quiet type. In fact one of his boyhood nicknames had been Noisy, a salute to his reticence. But he had a story, quite a story. He had spent the early years of his manhood suffering on the sandlots of America, playing semipro and minor league baseball, surfacing in the big leagues with the Philadelphia A's in 1944 for the proverbial cup of coffee.

Once he even brought in his scrapbook and his silver bat, the one he won in 1941 from the Louisville Slugger people for leading the minor leagues in batting average. It was the same year Ted Williams hit .408. Lefty had hit .453, and only a late-season slump dragged him down that low. He was a hitter, as all the newspaper clippings in his plump, weathered albums attested.

Lefty was always a joy to work with. He didn't care if we did our required floor-sweeping stint in the morning or not.

My father had a slogan: If you don't have something to do, find something to do. Lefty did: He'd tell stories.

My favorite story of his, from his ballplaying days, was about the night he was awakened in his hotel room by a couple of his teammates. The pitcher, a voyeur by avocation, had spotted a mating couple in the hotel across the way. So it was a hurried run to the roof of the hotel for a little peeping. It must have been some sight, a dozen minor league ballplayers, perched on the hotel roof, battling over who got the binoculars. "Finally the old catcher got his turn," said Lefty, stretching out his story for as much effect as possible. "And he's looking through them binoculars, watching that couple go at it, his tongue just a wagging. And finally it come out of his mouth, what he'd been trying to say. 'He's a southpaw,' he said."

With this Flick would let out a cackle. "That's the first thing a catcher'd notice. What hand he's using!"

That was the only baseball story I ever got out of Flick. Mostly he liked to talk about the other salesmen or the regular customers. I always wondered why he avoided the topic of baseball, why a man who spent fourteen years playing baseball never talked about baseball.

When I thumbed through his scrapbook, I marveled at his baseball accomplishments:

That silver bat.

A hit in each of his first three big league at-bats.

The batting championship of the top minor league, the American Association, while with the Milwaukee Brewers in 1945: a .374 average and 215 hits.

Ten All-Star seasons in the minor leagues.

Four minor league batting championships—'41 and '42 in the Appalachian League, '43 in the Inter State League, and '45 in the Class AAA American Association.

Thirteen .300 seasons in fourteen years of minor

league ball (1937–1951). He missed .300 by just .003 in 1939.

Perhaps his most amazing feat: the greatest one-day hitting spree any professional baseball player ever had. On July 21, 1946, Flick, playing for Little Rock of the Class A Southern Association in a doubleheader against Memphis, pounded out nine consecutive hits in his first nine at-bats, establishing a league record. He followed this accomplishment in the second game with a ground-out and then three more hits. All told he was twelve for thirteen that day, raising his batting average more than thirty-one points in what *The Sporting News* termed as the "best increase a player ever enjoyed in one day."

And yet it was like pulling teeth to get him to even allow as to how he had played in Milwaukee. He would shrug off his career by calling himself a "throw-in" in the George Kell deal, an allusion to the time he and future Hall of Famer—and his roommate—George Kell were traded to the big leagues.

Lewis Flick received no baseball pension. He received no bonus to sign a contract in 1935. All the money he earned in fourteen years of professional baseball was long gone by the time he came to work for my father. Lefty maintained no interest in the game after he left— he seldom watched a game on TV—and he never coached or offered any baseball instruction to youngsters.

I asked him once what happened. "I just got tired of it, so I quit. It just burned itself out in me, I guess."

Lefty is the best example I know of the wisdom: You never know who you're talking to. I'll bet in ten years of working with him, I only heard one person ever refer to his baseball career. He sure never brought it up.

He was just a guy in a checkered shirt asking, "Can I help you?"

Lefty died a couple of years ago. I didn't find out until I saw a small item in a national sports magazine. It was just a couple of sentences: his cup of coffee with the A's, his age, where he was living at the time of his death.

It didn't begin to capture the droll fellow I worked with on and off for a decade of my youth. I hope the few paragraphs in this book do.

PHILLIPS HEAD SCREWDRIVER—$2.98

Which came first: the Phillips head screw or the Phillips head screwdriver?

That's just an indication of the screwy questions they get at my local library. The answer to this one is easy, according to Claudia, my friendly librarian. The screw had to come first. There wasn't any need for the screwdriver until there was a screw. And another clue is the name of the company: Phillips Screw.

So the screw came first.

The Phillips Screw was invented by Henry F. Phillips of Portland, Oregon. It was first advertised in the November 7, 1935, issue of *Iron Age* in an ad for the American Screw Company. Phillips Screw Company trademarked the name Phillips Screw in 1938.

For many years Rule Industries owned Phillips Screw. It sold the company in 1993 for $4.5 million.

In the six decades since the Phillips Screw came into use, its parent company, Phillips Screw, has never manufactured a single screw or screwdriver. It only licenses Henry Phillips's patents.

If you grew up in the fifties you know that the Phillips screw was sometimes whispered to be part of the world communist conspiracy. It was in good company, with soccer and Elvis.

HERE COMES THE BRAD

While I'm loafing at Winfield Hardware, I thumb through a copy of *Chilton's Hardware Age,* the Bible of the industry. It's been around, under various names, for over a hundred years. My father got it when it was called just plain *Hardware Age.*

There's a cover story about how brides and grooms now register in hardware stores and why the industry should encourage it. The story even explains how to get more signups.

I show it to Ronnie. He just grins.

COTTER PIN—19 CENTS

I knew a guy named Cotter once, a bit of a prick, and I always thought the cotter pin was named for someone in his lineage. It's actually a shortened form of cotterel, the first name given to the pin fasteners. The word "cotterel" dates to at least 1570, when a "cotterelle" was mentioned in the *Louth Church Accounts*. It would be a hundred years before the name "cotter" showed up in written accounts.

The cotter pin is an ingenious little booger, sort of a safety pin without a sharp point. I use them all the time to fix stuff that keeps falling off my lawnmower.

1 Pound 10-Penny Common Nails—$1.09

What the hell, you may reasonably ask, is a ten-penny nail? Not that you don't already know. I mean, you know the size and the shape. You just don't know why it is called a ten-penny nail.

"Ten for a penny" is a good guess. But you won't get ten ten-penny nails for a penny at Winfield Hardware. You might have at my father's hardware store back in the fifties, when nails sold for nineteen cents a pound.

Actually, nails are sold by length. A ten-penny nail—which is written in hardwarese as "10d"—is three inches long. In England the "d" meant pound, not penny. Thus a thousand nails of this size (10d) weighed ten pounds. Somehow back in the Oliver Twist era, this got translated from pounds to pennies, making a ten-pound nail a ten-penny nail. It may have been that you could get ten 10d nails for a penny if your name was Uriah Heep. Since it probably isn't, you probably can't today.

Chapter 8
Wood and Wood Products

SOLOX USED TO BE MANUFACTURED for thinning shellac. To cut the shellac you needed a strong chemical, a very strong chemical. Like almost pure alcohol.

I learned many years ago at my father's store that thinning shellac is not all that shellac thinner is used for.

I had noticed that we had some regular Solox customers, derelict-looking fellows who would ask where the Solox was, buy a pint, and depart. But—hey!—half the guys who come into hardware stores are dressed like derelicts.

How was I to know there was more to the story?

My father finally confronted one of them, a sleepy-eyed regular. "What do you fellows do with Solox?" he asked.

The fellow seemed a bit spooked.

"I'm not gonna turn you in," my father promised.

"We drink it," the fellow admitted.

I ughed.

"Usually we mix it with orange soda," he volunteered. "That works best. Or hair tonic."

I ughed again.

"You ever have any problems with it?" my father continued.

"Nah. They say it'll make you go blind but it ain't happened to me."

We moved the Solox that afternoon. Back to the stockroom. My father—a teetotaling Gideon—was not about to let his hardware store become the liquor outlet for Kingsport's wino population.

The next time Sleepy came in for Solox I had to be the one to tell him we "didn't have any for him." That exact phrasing was my father's way of solving an ethical dilemma: lie about it or contribute to an alcoholic's downward spiral. *We didn't have any for him.*

When I told Ronnie my Solox story, he laughed. He'd been there.

"When I worked for Casto's Hardware, Mr. Casto said if you don't know them or if they don't look like a painter, don't sell 'em Solox. This one fellow came in and he looked like a painter so I sold him some. It happened that Mr. Casto was in the hospital at the time.

That night I went out to visit him and the guy I sold the Solox to was lying there on a stretcher. The orderly said they couldn't figure out what was wrong with him. I told them, 'I know what's wrong with him.' I never told Mr. Casto and I made sure I never sold it to anyone I didn't know again."

So the lesson is this: If you're ever in a hardware store, searching for the shellac thinner, and the clerk says simply, "Buddy, I can't help you," you might want to go home and look in the mirror.

You may look too much like a painter.

4-FOOT BY 8-FOOT SHEET ½-INCH PLYWOOD—$19.95

The father of plywood should have been John K. Mayo. In 1865 Mayo, a New York City inventor, received the first patent for a laminated wood panel. But Mayo never did anything with his patent and the unborn plywood industry remained unborn. Until 1905. That was the year of the Lewis & Clark Exposition at the Portland World's Fair (it was the one hundredth anniversary of Lewis and Clark's expedition).

For that expo the Portland Manufacturing Company, a wooden box factory, created laminated wood panels made from local fir and cheap glue. This "3-ply veneer work," as the company labeled it, was primitive in its manufacture. The company used its giant wood lathe to peel thin sheets of wood off a large log, spread glue across the veneer sheets with paintbrushes, and used house jacks to press it all together.

But several door manufacturers at the fair found this veneer product of interest and ordered plywood for their companies. By 1907 Portland Manufacturing had an automatic glue spreader, a sectional hand press, and orders for about 420 panels a day: almost all to door manufacturers.

The plywood industry was taking off. Or so it seemed.

Sales were healthy but not really growing.

The great boon to the plywood industry came in 1920 when Henry Ford began using plywood for the running boards on his cars.

By 1929 there were seventeen plywood mills in the Pacific Northwest, and production had reached an astonishing 358 million square feet a year.

But we all know what happened in 1929.

Crash! Wall Street Lays an Egg!

The Depression arrived, and by 1932 plywood production had plummeted to 200 million square feet a year.

Just when it looked darkest for the industry, in 1934 Dr. James Nevin, a chemist at Harbor Plywood Company, developed a fully waterproof adhesive.

Now plywood could be used for all sorts of exterior applications, including homes.

Soon plywood was everywhere. Admiral Richard Byrd built his huts at the South Pole out of plywood and carried his supplies in on plywood sleds. A plywood hydroplane won the President's Cup Race in 1938. Daredevil Norman Nevills rode 600 miles of Colorado River rapids in a plywood boat.

Then Pearl Harbor and Plywood Went to War. Barracks were made of plywood. Plywood PT boats patrolled the Pacific. Plywood gliders led the way on D-Day. The army crossed the Rhine in plywood assault boats.

Whew! This stuff was tough.

But the real boom lay ahead: the postwar housing boom. In the twenty years between 1934 and 1954 plywood production zoomed from 400 million square feet a year to 4 billion square feet.

And that was only the beginning. Builders began using it for residential home floors in 1955, and production doubled in the next five years, hitting 7.8 billion square feet in 1960.

Why? What is the attraction of plywood? Can't we just use solid wood?

Plywood is cheaper than regular wood because it is made from veneer strips peeled off logs. You could only get so many solid pieces out of the log, but by peeling wood strips, you can get almost down to the core.

And because layers are glued perpendicular to each other, plywood is stronger than regular wood. Wood is stronger along the grain and this cross-lamination distributes the wood's natural strength in both directions.

There's only one thing you have to know: Don't lay

plywood or any wood on the ground. It will warp. The sun will dry and shrink the top side, while the moisture from the ground will swell the bottom side.

3 Sheets Extra-Coarse (40 Grade) Aluminum Oxide Sandpaper—$1.89

The only reason sandpaper is called sandpaper is that it looks like sandpaper. It looks like someone has glued sand to paper.

But in the hardware industry it is called a "coated abrasive" and, technically, that's a more correct name. It's some sort of rough gritty material (an abrasive) and it is glued (coated) to a flexible, clothlike backing. And rarely is it sand and rarely is it paper.

I'm going to call it sandpaper in this section, rather than a coated abrasive, because in all my years working in hardware I never had a single customer come in and ask for a "coated abrasive."

Sandpaper traces its history back to the time when it was sand and it was paper, to thirteenth-century Asia where the Chinese glued sand and crushed shells and seeds to parchment.

As early as 1769 sandpapers were being sold on the streets of Paris. The first U.S. patent related to sandpaper was an 1835 patent for a machine that made sandpaper.

Sand is seldom used in sandpaper anymore. The most

common grits are flint, garnet, and the synthetics aluminum oxide and silicon carbide.

The major advantage of flint is that it's cheap; the major disadvantage is it doesn't last. Because flint particles are coarse they are easily dislodged from the backing. Professional woodworkers shy away from flint papers because they don't produce a good finish.

Garnet has a tougher grit than flint. Even though garnet paper is cheap, it's also good on wood.

But the most popular coated adhesives grit is aluminum oxide. It's a tough, hard synthetic that works equally well on wood, metal, or plastic; it has the added advantage of lasting longer than the natural abrasives flint and garnet.

Silicon carbide paper is tough and works well on wood, metal or plastic, even on wet surfaces. But it is much more expensive than the others and is generally reserved for a final polish.

Paper has fallen out of favor as a backing because it is thin and weak. Woven fibers such as cotton, polyester, or rayon and film are preferred as the backing for sandpaper.

If you've ever used sandpaper—and who hasn't?—you know that you don't just go into a hardware store and ask for sandpaper. Otherwise you'll be barraged with questions from the clerk. The most important will be: What grade of sandpaper?

Uh, huh?

Most folks entering a hardware store in search of

sandpaper use the primitive grading system: coarse, fine, etc. In actuality there are three different systems for labeling sandpaper according to its abrasiveness. Just what you need, another couple of systems to learn, right?

The basic system, the one everyone knows, describes the sandpaper in five simple terms: very coarse, coarse, medium, fine, and very fine. But hard-core woodworkers have found that labeling system too broad. They need more precision in their coated adhesives. So they developed what is called the aught or zero system. It starts with 2 for very coarse and goes down to 10 aught (written as 10/0), for very fine grit.

The third and newest system is the grit system, which starts at 32 for very coarse and runs to 600 for very fine, with a total of 16 grits.

You may also notice the term "open coat" on sandpaper. That means that just 70 percent of the backing is covered with abrasive. That wide spacing helps reduce clogging and the need for frequent replacements.

Sanding may be the most tiresome task in all of the do-it-yourself field. Back and forth, back and forth, push hard, but push consistently. And watch what you are doing.

There are modern power tools that take the drudgery out of sanding. The giant floor sander is one mother of a tool; my father rented them and when I was fifteen he let me try one out. That thing just tears up a floor. And that's the problem with all power sanders, even the hand models. They take out the drudgery but they also take out the precision. So on most sanding jobs the final sanding should be by hand.

My father used to offer his customers five simple sanding rules:

- Sand with the grain, not across it. Sanding across the grain will tear out hunks instead of small scratches.
- Use a sanding block. Keep the pressure even and the block straight and level, especially near the edge of your job.
- Start with a medium grit (in modern terms that's a 3/0 on the aught system or a 120 on the grit system) and gradually work up to a fine grit (7/0 or 240).
- Dust frequently so you can see where you are on your job.
- Hire somebody if you can afford it. Sanding is a bore.

Weather Stripping

Chapter 9
Building Supplies Department:
Caulks, Coatings, and Sealings

A SALLOW-FACED FELLOW under a Marshall University ballcap is building some shelves and has come in to buy angle iron. Ronnie leads him to the angle iron bin and proceeds to talk him out of buying any, actually talking himself out of a sale.

He convinces the fellow that he would be better off using two by fours and sends him down the road to the lumber yard.

"Well, can I buy some screws?" the amazed fellow asks.

"Naw. You don't have to do that."

Ronnie is convinced he did the right thing. "I could

have sold him that stuff, but he wouldn't have had a job when he got through. He wouldn't have been happy with it."

You don't get that kind of advice at the giant tool temples. But this is standard operating procedure at Winfield Hardware.

My brother-in-law Powell tells the story of the time he went in to buy a flanging tool. "I asked old Ronnie if he sold them. He said, 'I do but the ones I sell aren't worth a dime.' He said, 'Here take this one,' and loaned me the store's tool."

Another time Powell asked for some double-faced tape. "Ronnie said, 'I've got it but it's overpriced. I'd say go to Burdette's down the road.'"

"Service is what keeps us going," Ronnie tells me, explaining these incidents.

You won't see this in one of the big chains: a fellow in a blue Ferrelgas ballcap walks up to the counter, picks up the phone, and makes a call. No one asks if it's local or long distance or even related to his business in the hardware store.

You won't see this at the checkout counter either: Ronnie has already rung up a fellow's order. He has begun checking out the next customer, when the fellow holds up a roll of insulation: "Did you put that on there?" Ronnie shakes his head "no." "How 'bout this cable?" Again Ronnie shakes "no."

He wants the fellow to be able to get back to his job

so he says, "You just come back in later and tell me what you got."

When Ron is in the back, Randy takes me aside. "It's hard to tell how much he donates to local schools. He gives them all his mismixed paints. The football boosters, he just about built their new building.

"And somebody comes in and Ron knows they are going through hard times, he'll help 'em out. He'll give 'em a hot water tank and write it off. He still carries his electrical license. He'll go over and help 'em out putting it in."

My next-door neighbor Walter Shankel is the most cheerful weekend handyman I know. When he goes at a fix-it job, he has a method. He gets all the tools he thinks he'll need; he buys any parts he thinks necessary. And he whistles. He actually whistles while he works.

Perhaps more important, he takes his time.

I have never seen him in a hurry to fix anything.

He doesn't rush; he doesn't try to force anything (like a round peg in a square hole); and he doesn't get frustrated.

I, on the other hand, am more like my friend Sandi Bushnell's husband, Richard. She calls him a "negative handyman." "He's always getting mad when he fixes things. He's gotten really good at fixing jobs but he always gets angry when he works."

Been there, done that.

Example: When my son Will was three, he was visiting his grandma—my mother. She went to open the basement door and it stuck. "I've got to get that fixed," she told him. To which he replied: "I know how to fix things." He's three so she humors him. "You do? Well, how do you fix things?"

"You get a screwdriver and you throw it and you say, 'Dammit!'"

28-Inch by 34-Inch Sheet Single-Pane Glass— Out of Stock

Once my brother-in-law Powell Toth went into Winfield Hardware for a piece of glass. "I was framing a picture. I asked the clerk if they had a twenty-eight-by-thirty-four piece of glass. He said, 'Let me check.' He went running off to the back room. I could hear him back there: Zip—he was cutting a piece of glass, then . . . crash! Then a minute later: Zip . . . crash! And then another: Zip . . . crash! He comes back out and says: 'We don't have any.'"

Thompson's Wood Sealer Wood Preservative— $12.98

Bruce Haney and I are the reason hardware stores don't sell creosote anymore.

Now they sell all these prissy wood preservatives, but at my father's store, the wood preservative of choice was thick and black and smelly and cheap. It was called creosote and if you've never used any, you're not the Lone Ranger.

Most hardware stores don't sell creosote anymore.

Too dangerous.

Ronnie says to carry it he'd have to get a license and a million dollars in liability insurance and it's just not worth it. "I've found over the years that what the government don't outlaw, they license it so heavy you can't buy it."

My father sold it, though. Lots of it.

What is creosote?

The most common uses in the past have been on telephone poles, railroad ties, and boat docks. It's that oozy black stuff—it's made from tar—that seeps out. It's in a telephone pole to preserve it, make it resistant to water rot. Since most telephone lines are now strung underground and the railway system also is heading down, that leaves boat docks as the primary use for creosote.

I know all about that.

I never did know exactly what creosote was for . . . until I built a boat dock.

Technically, until Bruce Haney and I built a boat dock.

Bruce Haney is my best friend in the world. I may go months without seeing him or talking to him, but when we do get together, we can pick up just like it was yesterday.

We first met in the nursery at Sunday school, and over the years we worked on many projects together.

In the second grade we did a science project together. I'll never forget when our teacher, Miss Wilkinson, asked the class how it was that birds could sit on power lines without getting electrocuted. None of us had any clue—we were just seven years old. Then suddenly out of the mist of coughing and squirming, Bruce Haney raised his hand. "Miss Wilkinson," he began. "I think it's because birds have hollow bones."

Miss Wilkinson was taken aback. As the class gasped at little Bruce's brilliance, she stood numbly rocking from one foot to the other. But she was a college graduate—and an adult—and in a few seconds she recovered her composure and told us that, no, while Bruce had a good answer, it wasn't the right answer. Actually it was because the birds weren't grounded.

We went on with the rest of class. But for the rest of the year, we were all in awe of Bruce Haney. What an answer.

In reflecting back on this event, I have come to the conclusion that on that winter day in 1955, Bruce Haney invented bullshit. I'm pretty sure I'd never heard any before.

So in the seventies when I rented a lakefront house and decided I needed to built a boat dock, the first person I called was my scientific scholar friend Bruce Haney.

I named Bruce my project engineer. Any major home improvement project needs a project engineer. Someone to be in charge, to create a design, to plan where each nail goes. And, one hopes, to drive a few of those nails.

And Bruce is an engineer. OK, so he's a chemical engineer. He's still an engineer. And like Bruce said—if the boys down at the gas station can build a boat dock that works, he ought to be able to.

Next we needed a plan. So Bruce did some research. He visited other boat docks to see how the boys at the gas station had made theirs. He looked up the specific gravity of styrofoam. He calculated the weight of pine boarding. He figured. And ciphered. He drew. And sketched. And figured some more. He got estimates. And then he brought it over to my boat-dock-less lakefront house.

"Here it is," he said, handing me five pages of plans, including cross-sectional drawings, with little arrows telling what was what.

"How much will it cost?" I asked, getting to the heart of the matter quickly.

"Well, you got $380 in bolts and . . . $700 in lumber . . . and. . . ."

"Stop," I said. I couldn't sanction a boat dock that cost more than my boat.

So Bruce went back to the drawing board. A week later we had another meeting. This time there were only three pages of plans. And no cross-sectional drawings.

"What we've got here," began Bruce, "is a new concept in boat docks. It's called cheap."

"How cheap?"

"Well, you've got $25 in bolts, and . . ."

"When do we start?" I interjected.

Our next step was to buy the materials. Styrofoam

enough for an end-of-the-world floral arrangement. Bolts a foot long. Nails. Washers. Chain. Eyebolts. And, oh yes, lumber.

Now with lumber, you have a choice of lumber.

"What kind of lumber would you like?"

Well, just regular old lumber.

"OK, do you want fir-pine-oak-fiberboard-plywood-salt-treated-pine-or-what?"

Well, it's for a boat dock.

"Then you probably want salt-treated pine."

How much?

So after finding out how much, I settled for regular pine planking. This is where the creosote came in. Because I was too cheap to buy treated wood I had to buy a gallon of creosote. We would treat the wood ourselves, make it waterproof.

So after a trip to my father's hardware store—I got a discount there—Bruce and I were prepared to build.

Build? *Build?* Actually, very little of the time spent Building is spent *building*. Mostly it's spent sawing, painting, drilling, gouging, jury-rigging, poking holes; in general, tearing down. Everything must be torn apart before it can finally be put together to build something.

Our first project was sawing giant styrofoam logs. The trick with sawing styrofoam is not finding something to cut it—a butter knife will do that. The trick is finding something over twenty-four inches long to go through the entire width of it. A regular saw won't do. A bow saw gets hung up on the bow. After Bruce and I had made seventeen strategic cuts, none of which connected up, we started looking for a new cutter.

"I wonder if a wire would do it," Bruce mused.

"A hot wire would," I suggested.

"Tell you what," said Bruce. "If you'll hold the wire I'll stick it in the socket to get it hot."

While trying to remember the right-hand rule of currents and their fields, it struck me—there's an old cross-cut saw in the garage. I raced outside and triumphantly removed it from its dusty moorings, not noticing that a family of wasps had set up housekeeping on the handle. They were displeased at my attempt at wasp urban renewal and showed their displeasure to my collarbone and my stomach. These were the first Purple Hearts awarded during the boat dock construction. There would be more.

Our next step was to creosote the wood—for protection against rot. For this we enlisted the aid of our friend Robert. None of us had ever done any creosoting before, but we saw no reason why this would matter. We alternated using my one paintbrush—one of us would paint, two would lead cheers. It was during Robert's second turn that Bruce discovered the warning label on the creosote: "Do not get in contact with skin. Can cause severe burns."

But by this time we were all three thoroughly covered with creosote.

"Well, it can't be too dangerous or they wouldn't let them sell it," suggested Bruce. This was the seventies.

Robert and I agreed—hopefully. We broke up for the night and agreed to meet back bright and early the next morning to complete the building of the boat dock.

At seven on Saturday morning I was awakened by Bruce.

"Are you dying?" he asked, showing me his red face and arms. "I'm burning up."

Now that he mentioned it, I did seem to be dying. I went to the bathroom and saw in the mirror that my face was completely red and one eye had swollen shut. Bruce had two good eyes, but his nose was victimized. When Robert appeared, it was his chest and knees that were most affected.

We all decided that while we were dying, we might as well go ahead and finish the dock for future generations. Thus we drilled the wood, nailed on the planks, bolted on the styrofoam, and had it ready to put on the lake. Then we remembered. How are we gonna secure it to the shore? we asked in unison. Bruce, our project engineer, thought and thought.

"I've got it," he said. And then he proceeded to outline something about plumbing fixtures, pipe clamps, threaded steel rods, etc., etc.

We finally settled on rope and luck. We should have settled on a chain and lock. After we shoved the dock in the drink, roped it up, and had a drink back at the house, Bruce's wife, Rosey, came by to see how we were doing (aside from the creosote burns).

Bruce took her down to display our handiwork, and

found two little boys had cut the ropes and had the dock out in the lake paddling around. Five more minutes and all our creosote burns would have been in vain.

Using his best father figure voice Bruce calmly told the little boys that if they didn't get the dock back in where they found it, as they found it, he'd whip their bottoms real good. They claimed they thought the dock had just washed up. It did have that look about it.

They put the dock back where it had been—embarrassingly, they positioned it better than Bruce and Robert and I had—and we retrieved our tools from the house. We extended the ramp and built it around a tree. We figured anybody who wanted to steal a boat dock bad enough to cut down a twelve-inch-thick tree would probably rather steal a better boat dock.

Back at the house, we held an awards ceremony. Robert received a Purple Heart for his creosote burns; Bruce got two, one for his creosote burns and one for sitting in a cow pile while tightening a bolt; I got three, one for creosote burns, one for wasp stings, and one for falling off the dock as we positioned it on the shore.

But Rosey got the big award—the Most Valuable Player. If she hadn't come by and asked to see the dock, it would probably have floated to New Orleans.

And we all made a vow—never ever to use creosote again.

And I haven't.

Chapter 10
Door Accessories
Department:
Locks, Hinges

RON SAYS HE PRETTY MUCH has a lock—no pun intended—on the key-making business in town. "The pharmacy up the road has a key machine but they send their key business to me because they don't have anybody knows how to use the machine."

I know how. I started making keys at age twelve. The machines pretty much run themselves. The only trick is making sure you have the correct blank. Wrong blank and you'll never get the key to turn. Believe me.

Ron says his most popular blank is the KW-1 for a Kwikset door lock.

At my father's store the two most popular blanks

were B-10 and B-11. B-10 was the ignition key for General Motors cars, B-11 was for the trunk. I talked to the Curtis Key salesman who had my father's territory back in the sixties. He told me Curtis quit making B-10 and B-11 two years ago.

MASTER LOCK MODEL 15 — $6.99

If everyone were as honest as Abe Lincoln, there would never have been a need for locks. Locks are the ultimate symbol of human frailty.

But, hey, it didn't happen last week. Locks are as old as civilization. The ancient Egyptians invented the pin-tumbler lock and key, apparently to keep thieves out of their pyramid penthouses.

The lock itself was wooden and was fastened on the door. A bolt went through the lock and into a bracket on the wall. There were pins—made of either wood or iron, the Egyptians used both—that dropped into holes in the bolt, locking it securely. The key was nothing more than a piece of wood with pins that matched those in the lock. The pyramid-owner—or renter, as the case may have been—inserted this primitive key into a hole in the bolt and lifted up, disengaging the lock pins and opening the door.

The Greeks and Romans developed their own kinds of locks. The Greek key looked like a sickle, not exactly the handiest—or safest—thing to be carrying around.

The Romans used what is now called a warded lock—a projecting ridge on the lock or key permits only the correct key to be inserted. It worked, but when the barbarian hordes swept in, brute force was the rule and these prissy little locks were cute but no match for the boot of an enraged heathen.

But somehow in the march toward cable television, humans forgot how to make locks. And—amazing as it may sound—locks identical in form to those of the ancient Egyptians had to be reinvented in the Industrial Age.

The Art of the Locksmith, published in France in 1767, described the tumbler lock, so it has been in use for at least two centuries. Two decades later, in 1788, Englishman Robert Barron patented the double-action tumbler lock, with notches in the key that corresponded to the tumbler width. You'd get it all lined up, turn the key and—voilà!—the bolt moved. In all more than three thousand different kinds of locks were patented in England in the eighteenth and nineteenth centuries.

The combination lock was invented by the Chinese. But it didn't become popular until the 1800s when Jesse James and his friends discovered you didn't have to have a checking account to get money out of the bank. In 1873 a James Sargent patented an invention aimed at thwarting bank robbers: The timed combination lock meant the James Gang had to give up or spend the night in the bank because the lock could only be opened once a day.

But the main man of the modern lock industry, the inventor whose name has been associated with, or at least imprinted on, locks ever since, was Linus Yale, Sr.—Linus to his close friends, if he had any. After all, a guy who spends all his time inventing a lock is not the most trusting fellow.

In 1868 Yale reinvented the pin-tumbler lock, improving on the Egyptian models by using a revolving plug instead of a sliding bolt. Yale's pin-tumbler lock was innnovative in two ways. It was harder to pick and the key weighed only an ounce—before Yale locks, keys weighed a pound or more.

But Linus Yale's real genius was in the simplicity of his design and the fact that his locks could be manufactured on automatic machinery.

Yale was the name in locks for almost a hundred years, or until the invention of the TV commercial.

One sixty-second television commercial turned the tiny Master Lock company into the industry giant.

You know the commercial I'm talking about. A cop fires a bullet through a Master lock and it stays locked.

The original version of that commercial debuted on TV in 1965.

It was a .44 Magnum the gunman used. His bullet pierced the lock but it stayed snapped. It took a key to open it.

Master Lock came to television advertising out of necessity. Its patent for its padlock design—using layers of laminated steel instead of solid metal—had expired and Master needed a way to fight cheap foreign competitors.

The company had never advertised before that first ad. In fact, the president picked the ad agency out of the Chicago phone book.

Master Lock yanked the commercial after only a few showings. It seems people didn't believe it and were trying it at home. Master worried about the consequences. Not product liability—this was the sixties—the company just didn't want anyone getting hurt shooting at its locks.

The commercial, in an altered version, returned for the 1974 Super Bowl, this time using a rifle, because—the company reasoned—if people tried to copy the commercial, they wouldn't shoot at close range with a rifle.

That 1974 commercial was filmed at a shooting range in California's Tujunga Canyon. The rifleman fired at Master Lock Model No. 15, the same model lock used in the company's current commercials. The gunman shot forty locks; only three fell apart.

Master Lock used its entire 1974 TV ad budget on that one Super Bowl commercial. It paid $225,000 to air a commercial that cost only $10,000 to produce. And it worked.

Before that 1974 Super Bowl ad aired, Master Lock was a $35-million-a-year company. Today it sells more than $200 million worth of locks a year.

There are no Associated Press polls for lock makers, but industry publications estimate that Master Lock controls 60 percent of the market. It is number one.

A new version of the commercial is aired every year on the Super Bowl. Each time a rifleman fires through a Master Lock. And each time the lock jerks and spins but stays locked.

Just don't try it at home.

STANLEY 3-INCH T-HINGE—$5.98

The hinge was invented sometime back in antiquity. Its inventor never patented it, and even if he had the patent would have expired a millennium or so ago.

But one event took hinges out of the builders' supply warehouses and into the hardware stores. And that event occurred at Stanley's Bolt Manufactory, which was established in New Britain, Connecticut, in 1843 by Frederick and William Stanley.

There were scores of similar shops in Connecticut alone.

But the Stanleys were ingenious. They bought a single-cylinder high-pressure steam engine from a failed company so they could manufacture bolts, T-hinges, and wrought-iron straps more efficiently. They received a patent for the first hinge with ball bearings.

But the idea that made Stanley the name in cabinet hardware came from one William Hart.

Hart took over the presidency of the Stanley company after the Stanley brothers retired in the 1860s. It was Hart who decided that Stanley should package installation screws along with the hinge! What a bold idea! What a brave new world!

That something so simple as including screws with a hinge could alter an industry is unbelievable. But true. Stanley was the first company to do this. Others followed but Stanley was already in front. Still is.

Chapter 11
Adhesives
Department:
Tapes, Glues

THE STEREOTYPE OF A HARDWARE-STORE salesman is an old guy with a pocket protector full of pens in his shirt pocket and a knife and a measuring tape in his pants pocket. If he has one of those belt-loop key chains hung with keys, that's a plus.

Of course, it's not a stereotype.

There are plenty of old guys with pocket protectors clerking in hardware stores.

Why? Because people trust those kinds of guys in a hardware store. Anyone who fools with brackets and washers and strap hinges all day long knows more about hardware than the typical discount store clerk, who sells everything from milk to work clothes to as-pirin.

But there's also a place in the hardware store for young clerks, like Kenny. Kenny admitted to me that he finds something new every day in Winfield Hardware. "And I've been here almost three years!"

Young guys make up in energy what they lack in ex-perience.

The most energetic salesman I ever worked with at my father's store was a guy named Johnny. Johnny was an epileptic and the victim of blatant job discrimination, early sixties style. My father knew his father so one sunny morning Johnny reported for work.

Johnny was a go-getter who would rest against the front edge of the checkout counter and accost folks be-fore they had taken two steps inside the store. "Hep you?" he would ask, his mountain version of "May I help you?" Customers were taken aback. After all, they were scarcely inside the door and already a salesman was barking.

My father finally had to tell him he couldn't wait on anyone until he had reached the cash register itself. But my father's instructions didn't come until after Johnny had set what was undoubtedly the record for a sales pitch. Johnny was on his way to the café up the street for coffee—he was a good five steps out the door—when a man with heading-to-the-hardware-store written on his face approached. And there on the sidewalk, ten feet outside the door, under a clear blue sky, Johnny asked him: "Hep you?"

2-INCH BY 60-YARD ROLL DUCK TAPE BRAND DUCT TAPE—$4.99

Duct tape was invented in 1930 by Johnson & Johnson—the Band-Aid people—as a white waterproof cloth tape for use in hospitals. They called it Drybak. It didn't acquire its modern name and distinctive gray color until after World War II, when air-conditioning took off and sealing air-conditioning ducts became an occupation.

It was named duct tape.

Except you won't find one person in ten who calls it duct tape.

Most everyone calls it duck tape. In fact so many people call it that that one enterprising company—Manco, Inc., of Westlake, Ohio—sells its duct tape under the brand name Duck Tape.

Of course no one uses duct tape to tape ducts anyway. No one except air-conditioning installation guys.

I could probably write a book about the uses for duct tape and never once even mention ducts.

I fixed our patio door with it.

I used it to hold the head of my electric razor on.

I fixed my lawnmower gas tank with it.

I used it to get traction on the slick bottom of my rented shoes when my son got married.

My father-in-law used it to protect the body of an old car he had out in the backyard.

My son repaired an upholstered chair with it.

Last time I had some concrete work done the workers used it instead of gloves.

I know that beauty pageant contestants use it to give their breasts that perky look.

I know that rock music roadies use it to hold their spider's nest of mike and speaker wires together.

I know that stock car racers use it to streamline cracks on their cars.

And I know that Michael Dukakis's son used it to hold his father's hands firm to the podium during an important New Hampshire speech so the candidate wouldn't move them around so much.

Americans use 250 million square yards of duct tape a year.

How much is that? Well, if it takes a foot or so to reattach a floppy shoe sole, you could fix 13.5 billion shoes a year, a pair for everyone on the planet, and still have enough left over to repair a La-Z-Boy recliner.

But hardware stores sell duct tape for one purpose and one purpose only: to seal ducts. Officially.

SCOTCH TAPE—$1.19

There are water-sensitive tapes and heat-sensitive tapes but the type of tape most in use today is the pressure-sensitive tape. Push it on and it sticks.

The first adhesives were made from sticky things found in nature: tree sap, beeswax. In the Middle Ages animal tissues came into use.

Pressure-sensitive tapes are the result of scientists' trying to find new uses for rubber. Dr. Horace Day invented pressure-sensitive rubber tape for surgery in 1845. But since rubber is only sticky for a while, these early adhesive tapes needed other sticky agents—resins and oils, primarily.

Cars are responsible for the development of the first real adhesive tape. Two-tone models were popular in the twenties. But manufacturers couldn't get a sharp line betwen the two paint coats. They tried many solutions. Surgical tape didn't work because it took the paint with it when it was removed.

Minnesota Mining and Manufacturing got into the tape business when a lab worker named Richard Drew saw the need for a tape that would mask paint but still peel off easily during one of his auto plant visits to test sandpaper. He devised a paper-backed tape with rubber adhesive, a forerunner of masking tape.

He didn't call it Scotch tape: That name came from a customer. And while the story about the origination of the name Scotch tape isn't politically correct, neither are most hardware stores.

One of the first batches of Drew's tape didn't get a full coat of adhesive. A painter complained to his sales rep about 3M's "stingy Scotch bosses." They liked the name because it signaled an economical product. And thus was born Scotch tape.

Rubber is no longer used as the adhesive in tape. Modern tapes use adhesomers, synthetic polymers, that are naturally—if a synthetic can be called natural—sticky.

Most tapes are manufactured in wide, wide, rolls, then sliced into smaller widths.

Adhesive tapes had sales of $6.5 billion in 1990. That is one heck of a lot of money for a product whose sole purpose is to stick things together that aren't supposed to be stuck together. Sort of like marriage.

.07-OUNCE TUBE DURO SUPER GLUE—$1.19

Glue is not new. Humans have been bonding things with sticky saps since the dawn of time. (Actually half past the dawn of time: It was too dark at the dawn itself.) But the glue industry didn't take off until the first half of this century. Three things fueled that rapid growth: the burgeoning plywood industry, which needed glues to bond wood slabs together; the development of synthetic adhesives, which were stronger and cheaper than natural glues; and World War II, when Americans knew that the only way to beat Hitler was to glue him to his homeland. Actually the Armed Forces needed glues for all manner of uses.

There are a slew of glues, but the most amazing one is the one you and I call super glue. Chemists call it cyano-acrylate glue, or C.A.'s for short. And it was invented—discovered is a better word—in my hometown, not three miles from my father's hardware store.

Super glue was discovered at Eastman Kodak's Kingsport, Tennessee, plant in 1951 by Dr. Harry Coover and Dr. Fred Joyner, who were trying to determine how much light was refracted by a piece of ethyl cyanoacrylate film. When they couldn't get the film out of their refractor, they concluded they had ruined their expensive piece of scientific equipment, not that they had discovered a new super kind of adhesive.

Kodak began selling Eastman 910—their name for super glue—in 1958. The company no longer sells it; Kodak decided a few years back to concentrate on what it knew best, photography and fabric (Kodel) and a few other lines, and leave glue to the glue magnates.

Normal glues are sort of a subatomic version of Velcro, grabbing by the hook and eye principle. But not super glue. In fact no one really knows how it works. There is speculation that perhaps it is an electromagnetic attraction.

With regular glue, the thicker the application the better, but it's just the opposite with super glue. A thin film works better than a thick one.

Model airplane glues and the like are packaged in metal tubes but you can't package super glue in metal tubes because it reacts with them.

Ronnie sells super glue remover, " 'cause some sucker's going to glue his fingers to the countertop."

Chapter 12
Lawn and Garden Department:
Lawn Tools

THERE'S MORE SOLD AT THE HARDWARE STORE than just hardware. Entire businesses are bartered and traded and sold.

There was one customer today that Ronnie had been looking for all week.

"Wayne, how you doing?" Ronnie greeted him.

"Piddling around. I just like to piddle."

"I heard you're gonna get out of the sawmill business. The reason I ask is I had a fellow say he wanted to buy it."

At this the fellow with Wayne bolts up to the counter. "I got a mill at Bronco Junction."

There's no sale this time, but Ronnie says this is not an uncommon occurrence at Winfield Hardware.

"A guy came in and wanted me to figure out what a hardware store he wanted to buy was worth. So I give him a figure of two hundred thousand dollars. He said they wanted five hundred thousand dollars. I told him if you want to pay half a million for a hardware store come and see me."

Owning a hardware store is the pipe dream of countless American men. For most, it remains in the pipe, with all the other smoke they blow.

But a few act on that impulse.

So you think you want to open your own hardware store?

Maybe you should talk to Ronnie Matthews first. "Hey, this one might be for sale."

After my father died, I found an old U.S. Department of Commerce pamphlet in his papers, a guide to opening your own hardware store.

The booklet is called *Establishing and Operating . . . A Hardware Store* and it was published in 1946.

This government publication has a checklist of the personal qualifications you need—or needed in 1946—to open your own hardware store. See how you stack up.

Have you had previous experience in this line of business?

Have you ever bought merchandise before?

Do you know the characteristics of the merchandise you will handle?

Do you have the special technical skills which are needed?

Have you ever supervised the work of others? Been boss?

Have you ever hired people? Met a pay roll?

Have you ever dealt with the public? Do you like to meet people?

Have you ever sold?

Can you boss yourself? Drive yourself to do what is necessary? Are you a self starter?

Do you have imagination? Energy? Initiative?

Are you willing to work long hours?

Can you overcome obstacles? Fight down discouragement? Keep plugging?

Have you considered working for someone else to get more experience?

There is no correct score—you don't have to answer "yes" to at least half to qualify to start a hardware store. But the questions should give you an idea of the character traits you need in order to succeed in the fast-paced world of hardware.

The book offers a list of tools the budding hardware-store owner needs to stock "to produce $1,000 annual sales." The dollar figure is way off for today but the list is still solid: auger bits, non-ratchet braces, chalk, chisels, clamps, concrete tools, wing dividers, drills, screwdrivers, wire fencing tools, files, grinders, hammers, handles, hatchets, levels, mallets, nail sets, nippers and pinchers, pencils, planes, pliers, punches, rules, saws, saw blades, saw sets, snipe, square, sharpening stones, measuring tapes, blowtorches, trowels, bench vises, and wrenches.

The pamphlet also suggested stocking three kinds of goods:

- Convenience goods—"things the consumer wants to purchase with the least possible effort." In hardware that's electric lightbulbs, nails and tacks, small tools.
- Shopping goods—things "the customer buys only after comparing them for suitability, quality, price and style." In hardware this is appliances, costly tools, and machines.
- Specialty goods—things "he insists on getting and will go out of his way for." A washing machine was an example in 1946.

The government even offered helpful tips on finding a location. The key, according to the pamphlet, was traffic count—how many people walked by the store. "A town of less than 100,000, the down town district had 4,100 passersby per day and 15 percent of them entered the establishment. A side street had 1,800 passersby daily with 22 percent coming in." The lesson is stay on Main Street: 15 percent of 4,100 is 615; 22 percent of 1,800 is only 396.

For the prospective hardware man or woman who passed the suitability test, bought the right inventory, and located in the proper spot, the government had good news: "The hardware store that stays in business for five years has a life expectancy of about 25 years. Of stores opening in 1930 46 percent of hardware stores were still in business, second only to drug stores with 50 percent."

In 1955 *Changing Times* magazine offered its own guide to opening your own hardware store. (Recall that was the year my father went into the hardware business.)

Changing Times said the average capital investment for a hardware store was forty-five thousand dollars, with twenty thousand dollars the minimum. I know that my father and his partner opened that year with ten thousand dollars.

Changing Times also cautioned against opening "without some knowledge of retailing, better, of course, to have worked in a hardware store."

In the ten years since the government's pamphlet, the hardware business had become specialized. *Changing Times* identified four distinct types of hardware stores: "the residential store (ma-and-pa) specializes in household items; the downtown version (one or two man shop) serves nearby business needs; the suburban location (3–5 employees) serves householders; rural stores carry builders hardware, fencing, roofing and agricultural supplies."

The magazine also recognized the importance of location: "Get on the busiest side of the busiest block, better if near a flourishing grocery store. A shopping center is [a good] choice. . . . Make sure there's ample parking."

Changing Times even offered a starting budget:

Furniture fixtures	$3,000
Cash register, scales	300
Misc. painting constr.	200
Extra help	300
Rent advance	200
Insurance	200
Accounting records	80
Stationery, office supp.	50
Misc. store supplies	100
Advertising	170
Owner's living expense (one month)	250
Petty cash	150
Cash for opening stock	15,000
TOTAL	20,000

SALES BUDGET

Sales	50,000
Cost of goods sold	35,300
Owner's salary	3,800
Other salaries	5,050
Advertising	700
Contributions	50

Delivery expense	300
Depreciation	350
Utilities	375
Insurance	375
Interest	50
Losses on accounts	75
Office supplies, postage	175
Rent	1,225
Repairs	50
Taxes	525
Telephone	150
Other, including store supplies	500
NET PROFIT	1,650

Changing Times also had good news for the prospective hardware man or woman. "The hardware business has the lowest mortality rate of all retail stores."

Those are numbers from almost a half century ago. Ronnie Matthews is reluctant to open his books to the entire free world and I don't blame him. He told me how much business he does in an average year and I told him I wouldn't print it.

But for a little real-world economics, here's what my father's figures were for the last full year his store was in business, July 1, 1982, to June 30, 1983. These numbers are just a little over a decade old, but from conversations with a few hardware folks, they work for today's store, too.

My father would want me to tell you that this was his

last year and his worst year. He was not actively involved in the store at the time and sales had fallen off.
Five years earlier he had bigger sales, much bigger sales.

TOTAL SALES	$146,311.67
Purchases	89,984.48
GROSS PROFIT ON SALES	56,327.19
OPERATING EXPENSES	
Wages	33,172.37
Officer's salary	6,000.00
Contract labor	88.00
Rent	5,985.00
Supplies	266.66
Utilities	3,084.33
Advertising	324.01
Office expense	583.52
Telephone	581.17
Employee relations	26.59
Insurance	5,488.19
Payroll taxes	3,601.81
Taxes & licenses	377.51
Accounting	905.00
Cash short/over	398.30
Depreciation expense	12.87
TOTAL OPERATING EXPENSES	60,895.33

That gave his hardware business a loss of $4,568.14
for the year. He had retained earnings from previous

years so he didn't have to dip into his own pocket to pay the loss.

I think most of the categories are self-explanatory. "Contract labor" was what he paid a couple of neighborhood teenagers to come in and take inventory. "Advertising" was for buying matches with the store name imprinted. That and the local high school yearbook were his only forms of advertising. I have no idea what "Employee relations" means. Perhaps he bought a wedding present for one of his clerks.

So now you can go open your own hardware store.

Or you could go talk to Ronnie Matthews, make him an offer.

BOOK OF MATCHES WITH WINFIELD HARDWARE IMPRINTED ON THE COVER—FREE TO CUSTOMERS

Like many great inventions, the match was an accident. British pharmacist John Walker was working in the lab in 1826 when he stirred a mixture of potash and antimony with a wooden stick. When he couldn't get the gob of mix off the stick, he rubbed it on the floor. And— bam!—fire!

Wow!

He recognized immediately what he had. No more rubbing sticks together for hours on end. No more carrying coals from one house to another.

He began manufacturing matches the next year, using prison labor from a local almshouse. After some experimenting with the packaging, he settled on a pasteboard box with a strip of sandpaper enclosed for striking.

But Walker never patented his invention—concentrating instead on his drug business and leaving advances in matchmaking to others.

An American attorney named Joshua Pusey invented the matchbook, patenting it in 1892. He licensed his invention to the Diamond Match Co. of Barberton, Ohio. The Diamond folk soon recognized the possibility of using the matchbook cover for advertising and in 1898 they sold the first matches with advertising covers to the Mendelson Opera Company.

50-Foot ⅝-Inch Swann Garden Hose—$12.98

People used to water their gardens and lawns with a sprinkling can. I can remember the old woman who lived two doors from us out in her sunbonnet dribbling water into each and every garden plant. It was her choice. The garden hose was ubiquitous by the fifties.

It was rubber garden hose that effectively launched the rubber industry.

Rubber, like the turkey, is one of those indigenous American products that went to Europe and then came back. American Indians made balls out of rubber and Columbus—the guy who thought he had found China when in fact he had found a Caribbean resort—carried these rubber balls back to Spain. It was a neat little toy but no one could come up with any other uses for rubber. It was too brittle when it was cold and too sticky when it was hot.

Rubber was tamed by an American, who goofed in his kitchen.

The man's name—and you've heard it before in conjunction with rubber—was Charles Goodyear, a tinkerer, who thought he could cure rubber like he cured leather. He was playing around in his kitchen during the winter of 1839, experimenting with various rubber compounds, trying to find just the right chemical to cure rubber. He mixed up sulfur and rubber, then accidentally dropped a spoonful on the stove. He was too absorbed to clean up the mess, figuring, as most men in the kitchen do: "I'll clean it up later."

When he did return to it later, it had cooled and dried and he liked what he found: It wasn't sticky or brittle, but smooth and flexible. He put a piece outside in the winter cold. The next morning he was ecstatic. It was still flexible. It was . . . rubber!

Goodyear had accidentally stumbled onto the process of vulcanization and he spent the rest of his life—and all his money—trying to perfect the process. He ran out of money and died penniless—actually less than penniless: He died two hundred thousand dollars in debt.

It was left to the similarly named Benjamin Franklin Goodrich, an Akron, Ohio, doctor, to finish the vulcanization research. Goodrich saw a need for a rubber hose—he had watched a friend's house burn to the ground after a leather fire hose burst—so he put together a group of investors and started a company to devise rubber goods. In 1870 the B. F. Goodrich Company began selling rubber hose.

And that's why Akron is called the Rubber City. And Goodrich is more famous than Goodyear. Except in the world of blimps.

ORTHO WEED-BE-GON WEED KILLER—$6.98

Weed killer is another miracle product that I don't understand.

Just by spraying a little mist out over my lawn (grass and weeds mixed in there), I can effectively send the weeds packing, leaving a luxurious green carpet.

What I don't understand is how the weed killer knows which is the weed and which is the grass. How does it know the difference?

So I called my old buddy Bob Hill, who's been writing a gardening column since before I even owned a lawn. Every couple of years Bob and the local TV gardening guy, Fred Wiche, publish a gardening almanac that sells like crazy. I own a copy, out of my sense of obligation to my friends to buy their books, but I have no intention of ever doing any more serious gardening.

I read through the entire book and nowhere do Bob and Fred explain how weed killer knows the difference between grass and weeds.

So that's how I came to call Bob. How do weed killers

know the difference between weeds and grass? He didn't even hesitate. "They go to school."

In other words, he didn't know either. "But that's my answer and I'm sticking to it."

He did suggest that if I wanted a different answer, I might call 1-800-ORTHO. That's about two digits short of a phone number but I looked on my bottle of Weed-Be-Gon and got the complete Ortho hotline: 1-800-225-2883. The number 225-2883 doesn't spell ORTHO. In fact I got sidetracked trying to figure out what it does spell. Fortunately, I had plenty of time while I was on hold, waiting for the next available representative.

1-800/BAL-CUTE?

1-800/ABL-A-TUF?

1-800/BAK-A-TUF?

1-800/BAK-A-VUE?

So how does Weed-Be-Gon know the difference between grass and weeds?

"It's selective," according to the Ortho lady, who didn't know what 225-2883 spelled either. "It doesn't kill blade-type plants. It kills just broadleaf weeds. It is absorbed by certain types of plants, broadleaf. And not grasses."

I think the key was the last thing she told me: "We tested it and it killed broadleaf weeds but not blade-type grasses."

Pretty much like every other great invention in this book. Someone stumbled onto it and was smart enough to recognize what he had.

Back to the important stuff:
1-800/BAJA-VUE?
1-800/BAJA-TUE?
I give.

Prozap Mouse Maze — $4.99

What was it that Ralph Waldo Emerson promised? Build a better mousetrap and the world will beat a path to your door?

I'm not sure I want the world to beat a path to my door. Do I have to pave it? And if I don't, who's going to pay for the grass seed to resod my yard? And the fertilizer and seed-spreader rental? Not to mention liability insurance.

But it is true that the world has been trying to build a better mousetrap since the first mousetrap patent was granted back in 1838. Literally, the world has been trying: there have been almost 5,000 mousetrap patents granted in this country since then and new applications come into the Patent Office at the rate of about 75 a year.

I caught a glimpse of the latest "better mousetrap" at the National Hardware Show in Chicago.

If the National Hardware Show sounds like every guy's dream convention, it's because you haven't been.

The show isn't populated with hardware guys—old-timers with pocket protectors and a lifetime of experience fixing stuff. It's filled with suits—aggressive young salesmen angling for promotions. There are a lot of hardware guys walking around, inspecting the tool displays and fake ceramic bathrooms. But there are also a lot of buyers from the big chains, all being chased by salesmen from the big manufacturers.

The National Hardware Show—which is a registered trademark of the American Hardware Manufacturers Association—has been held since 1945. It's a gathering of seventy thousand buyers and sellers in the hardware business.

My favorite part of the show was the "better mouse-traps" display: the New Products Expo.

The New Products Exposition featured eleven hundred new hardware items.

There was a carbon monoxide detector that runs on electricity instead of batteries, for those of us who are too stupid to change the battery every New Year's Day. And when I say "those of us," I mean me. I change them when they start chirping.

There was an alarm for when the water rises above your basement sump pump.

There was a voice-activated dog collar to train your pet.

And a garden hose brush for cleaning barbecue grills.

There were Christmas light holders for your roof and a lightbulb that dims after dark to become a night light.

I examined a wall-hugging extension cord and a four-way plug that allows you to hook up four garden hoses to one faucet.

The New Products Expo is the place where Gyro Gearloose–type inventors unleash the gizmos that they hope will take off like The Club did.

My favorite New Product, as it turned out, really was a better mousetrap.

The latest "amazing new discovery in mouse control," announced in a press conference at the show, was the Prozap Mouse Maze from Hacco, Inc. Hacco is, of course, the "leading contract manufacturer and developer of pesticide bait technologies and formulation."

And you didn't even know there was a field called "bait technology."

The Mouse Maze is a patented device—it looks sort of like a tract home for mice—that attracts mice with its "desirable food source." That desirable food source—as anyone who watches Road Runner cartoons suspects—is actually a mouse pesticide.

So mice enter by any of three doors—okay, "check in." The entryways are designed as "simulated burrow openings" so mice actually do think it is a mouse motel. They eat that desirable food source. And die. Right there inside the Mouse Maze. The Mouse Maze will hold "up to four mice" or up to four dead mice, if you prefer. As soon as it fills up, you just throw it away. Or as soon as it stinks.

Actually Ralph Waldo Emerson didn't say "build a better mousetrap and the world will beat a path to your door." In his journal in 1855 he wrote, "If a man has good corn, or wood, or boards, or pigs, to sell, or can make better chairs or knives, crucibles or church organs, than anybody else, you will find a broad hard-beaten road to his house, though it be in the woods." Thirty-four years later, in the book *Borrowings,* editors Sarah Yule and Mary Keene misquoted him: "If a man can write a better book, preach a better sermon, or make a better mousetrap than his neighbor, though he builds his house in the woods, the world will make a beaten path to his door."

So it wasn't Emerson who inspired the four thousand mousetrap patents of the last century and a half, it was Sarah Yule and Mary Keene. Yule and Keene and the fact that Americans spend $300 million a year in rodent control. I suspect that dollar figure may have much more to do with it than anything any dead poet never said.

MTD 21-INCH LAWN MOWER—$229.95

I got a clipping in the mail the other day from my high school pal Bruce Haney—just a clipping, with the notation: "Show this to Judy." Judy is my wife. The clipping detailed how a guy in my hometown—I didn't know him although he was my age—had met his end: a massive heart attack while mowing the lawn.

Bruce knows I hate mowing and he thought I might want to use our friend's untimely end as an excuse to get out of mowing.

I tried.

I'll use any excuse: heat, humidity, wet grass (it'll tear up the lawn mower), dry grass (it'll die if I clip it), national holidays.

I keep thinking that if I let it grow long enough, maybe some government agency will step in and declare my backyard a wildlife preserve.

I was born under a bad lawn mower sign.

No matter what kind of lawn mower I buy—cheap or expensive; name brand or no brand; new or used—it breaks.

So I gave up on expensive, name brand, and new. I buy what my lawn mower man Lew Tabor calls "Target mowers." By that he means those no-name cheap mowers that discount stores like Target and Kmart set out front with attractive prices plastered all over them.

I go Lew one better. I don't even buy them at Target. I buy them used from someone who bought them at Target. My present lawn mower I bought at a *yard* sale—I thought that was an appropriate place to buy a lawn mower. In fact, I didn't even *buy* it. I traded my neighbor Bill Kite one of my books *(Can You Trust a Tomato in January?)*: a twenty-dollar book for a twenty-dollar lawn mower.

The book lasted longer than the lawn mower. I'm sure of that. Remember, I'm the guy born under the bad lawn mower sign.

I had the lawn mower for a year before it broke. I took it in to Lew Tabor, who took one look at it and laughed. He always laughs at my lawn mowers.

"What's wrong with it?" he asked. I pointed to the pull rope, which was hanging out like a dog's tongue on a hot day. He tugged on the cord, but the lawn mower was not interested in sucking the cord back in.

"What's it doing?" he asked.

That's the hardest question a mechanically inclined person can ask a non–mechanically inclined person. It leads to grown men exchanging grunts and chirps and other sound effects. "It sounds sort of like this: Gr-i-i-i-i!" I said.

"When did that start?"

"Right after it went gu-rung-rung-rung!"

"What did you do before that?"

"Uh, that was when I ran over that tree stump that I couldn't see for the high grass."

That's when Lew's lightbulb went on: "Did it squeal?"

"As a matter of fact it did."

"I can fix it."

We agreed that he would not invest more than twenty-five dollars of his time and parts. That would still be five dollars more than I had in the mower.

As of this writing my little used Target mower is puttering away, chopping off the grass and making me feel like a contributing member of suburban society.

The history of the lawn mower is tied inexorably to the history of the lawn.

Cochise, for instance, didn't have a lawn mower and didn't need one. He didn't have a lawn. Or more precisely, the entire state of Arizona was his lawn.

Before the Industrial Revolution, about the only folks with lawns were also the only folks with land: the super rich. In the Middle Ages shortened grass was popular for picnic areas, sporting events, and gardens. The lawn effect was achieved by pounding the grass down with mallets. The first great advancement in lawn mowing came with the invention of the scythe.

One of the earliest mentions of lawn mowing is credited to Sir Francis Bacon, the English essayist and statesman, who in the sixteenth century praised "closely mown lawns because nothing is more pleasant to the eye than green grass finely shorn." Later that same century, in 1664 to be precise, British horticultural writer John Evelyn told his readers that lawn areas should be mowed every fifteen days.

Of course neither Bacon nor Evelyn had "shorn" their own grass. That was left to the hired hands. One hired hand could hand-cut a quarter-acre of grass in about three hours with a scythe. Then a team of servants required another two or three hours to sweep up the grass.

The Great Leap Forward, when it comes to lawn mowing, occurred in 1830. Edward Budding, the foreman at a Gloucestershire, England, textile mill, had invented a cutting machine to shear the nap off velvet. One day while watching his machine work, he had one of those Eureka moments: This could be adapted to shear the grass off the lawn!

In his patent for that first lawn mower Budding declared, "Country gentlemen may find, in using my machine themselves, an amusing, useful and healthy exercise."

The first Budding machine was an early variation on the reel lawn mower, nineteen inches wide and pushed from behind (by a man in a top hat and tails, if you believe the first ads). It was sold in England by Ransomes department store for the steep sum of seven guineas (about the same price as a mail-order bride). Soon the Budding machine was available in a variety of sizes, all of them troubled by a problem known to modern man: salesman overhype. The salesman might tell a purchaser it was a one-man mower but by that he meant one NFL lineman. An 1868 issue of *Gardener's Chronicle* magazine recommended, "It would be as well to purchase a boy's size for a man, while a ladies' size is probably best for a boy."

The first American version of the lawn mower was the "Archimedean," named for the Greek mathematician, who, we noted earlier, had a lot to do with the invention of the screw. The Archimedean had the advantage of employing a single blade and the disadvantage of being noisier than all get out. No one in the house could carry on a conversation while the lawn was being mowed.

Soon the lawn mower was a staple of city life. The Geneva County (New York) Horticultural Society reported in 1870 that 150 lawn mowers had been sold that spring in Rochester alone. "Yet five years ago, or even less, outside of some half a dozen places, there was not a square rod of lawn about the city."

There were even lawn-mowing competitions, including one at the famous Paris International Exhibition of 1889. The winner mowed down sixteen hundred square feet in six minutes and thirty-five seconds.

Power mowers hit the market in 1893, and boy were they an immediate hit, even if the first ones were steam-powered, weighed a ton and a half, and lacked any semblance of maneuverability. Gas-powered mowers were introduced in 1902.

Today a lawn mower is a necessity—like a TV, it's on the government's poverty list. That's happened rather rapidly: three generations in my family. My grandmother used a cow for her mowing. She had a farm with a tiny farmhouse and fenced yard in the middle of her spread. Once a week or so she would let Bessie, the most docile of their cows, into the yard, to chew up the grass.

When my parents married, they left farm life behind and moved to the city. And bought a little reel push mower. It derived its force from the person pushing it. The blades were mounted horizontally and as the wheels turned, so did they.

I remember when our next-door neighbor, Walter Shankel, bought a gas-powered reel mower in 1954. He was the envy of every sweaty kid in the neighborhood. Not only was his mower motor-powered, it was self-propelled! He just walked along behind it, guiding it.

By the end of the fifties, every house on my block had a gas-powered lawn mower. And now the rotary blades had been replaced by one large horizontal blade. That's how I earned spending money in junior high, mowing lawns.

I'd like to say that today when I push my little Target mower around my yard it takes me back to my early days of entrepreneurship and I get a warm glow. Mostly I get a sweaty brow and tired legs.

I'll bet over the course of my life I have walked a thousand miles behind lawn mowers. And I haven't enjoyed a single second of it.

But I have figured out a few things; I call them the Laws of Lawn Mowing:

1. *The lawn mower always runs out of gas at a point equidistant from the gas can and a cold beer.* Talk about decisions. Do I finish the lawn? Or do I start the beer?

2. *Grass grows in inverse proportion to how busy you are.* Just when you have the least time to mow, that's when the yard grows like a rain forest.

3. *Lawn mowers take as long to repair as you want them to.* I guess that's what I like about my lawn mower man, Lew Tabor. When my mower quits—an event that happens at least once a mowing season—I'll take it in and he'll tell me confidently, "I'll try to squeeze you in in the next couple of days." Then when I get ready to mow again—an

event that can take up to two weeks—I'll give him a call. "It'll be ready tomorrow."

4. *The grass is always greener if you have a chemical lawn service.* Humorist Erma Bombeck had a best-seller in the eighties with a book titled *The Grass Is Always Greener over the Septic Tank.* That tells me that Bombeck is familiar with the pull-rope end of a lawn mower. But sadly the title is dated. Septic tanks have gone the way of push mowers, which is to say, you still see a few of them, but nobody who has one really wants one.

And the days of getting a little aerobic exercise fighting dandelions one at a time with a squirt bottle of weed killer have been replaced by the days of aerobic check writing to a professional chemical lawn service.

I don't use a chemical lawn service anymore. I used to but I got a little nervous about it when our cat died mysteriously two days after a lawn spraying. We didn't have an autopsy. It wasn't like I was going to sue the lawn service for the loss of affection of my cat. To win a judgment on that one you'd have to find a jury of twelve people who had never owned cats. But I always thought there was a connection. So I dropped chemical lawn services. My neighbors didn't, which means it drives all the weeds to my lot.

Chemical lawn services give you a green carpet for a lawn but they also give you a season of endless mowing because of all the fertilizers they put in.

So when it comes to lawns and lawn mowers, I am strictly low-tech: my Target mower chops down dandelions and clover and occasionally a speck of grass.

I like it that way.

Today there are five million acres of lawns in this country. Americans spend about $6 billion annually keeping them looking nice. There really is no secret to having a lawn that looks like green carpet. It's as well-known as the old joke about the American tourist who inquired of the gardener at an English country home how he got the lawn looking so grand. "Nothing to it, sir. You mow it and roll it for about three hundred years."

WEED EATER—$119.98

I don't remember life before hammers or nails or even the Phillips screwdriver. But I can remember life before the Weed Eater. It was back-breaking and knee-bruising and hand-callusing. You'd have to squat down with those little grass snips and snip-snip-snip, pretty much blade by blade, the grass in those hard-to-cut spots.

Then came Thomas N. Geist and George C. Ballas.

They too were tired of squatting and snipping.

The difference between them and everyone else is they did something about it.

They invented the Weed Eater.

It was 1971 when Texans Geist and Ballas patented their "improved cutting assembly for rotary lawnmowers, edgers or the like."

Their device included "a body member arranged for rotating about an axis normal with the cutting plane. At least one cutting line is attached to the body member for rotation therewith in the cutting plane. . . . The cutting lines are preferably nonmetallic so as to reduce the hazardous condition which would otherwise be present for the operator and still provide an apparatus which will cut with great efficiency and safety."

What does that mean? How was it different? Read on in the patent—the historic patent: "Heretofore, the rotary head, or cutting blade of rotary lawnmowers, edgers and the like have comprised a rotating metal bar. . . . However such bars create hazardous conditions in that when they strike certain objects they . . . create and project dangerous missiles which may strike the operator or individuals in the area of work."

The Weed Eater was revolutionary in that it cut grass with something that wouldn't cut your hand or foot (sting maybe): fishing line. And that cutting edge could be easily replaced when it wore out: You just reeled out more line.

SWING SET: SOME ASSEMBLY REQUIRED—$229.95

The next time I buy a house, remind me to look in the backyard first.

If there isn't a swing set embedded in concrete (so the owners can't take it with them), I'm not signing the contract.

I don't care what brand it is. The best swing set isn't necessarily the one from Wood Play or Hedstrom or Child Life.

The best swing set is the one that is already assembled.

I learned that lesson the hard way, by assembling one on a recent weekend, or, technically, a weekend and a half.

Will, my five-year-old, had been asking for a swing set since before Christmas. In a moment of credit-card weakness, I told my wife to go ahead and order it and put it on our charge card.

It was delivered Friday afternoon, just in time for the weekend. It came in a box twelve inches high, eighteen inches wide, and fifteen feet long. The bag of nuts and bolts weighed as much as Will.

"We'll get started on it tomorrow morning," I told Will in my best Ward Cleaver voice.

Saturday morning Will was up bright and early, kneeling by the bed. "Daddy, when are you going to put my swing set together?"

"Let's wait till it's light out," I replied.

When I assemble a toy, I usually prefer to use an instruction manual as a last resort. But once I peeled the cardboard packing off, I knew this was going to be different.

Will immediately began sorting the parts out for me, using his own sorting method: big and little. Big pieces here and little pieces over there.

I sat down and began reading. The instruction manual was written by someone for whom English was a third language (Japanese was first, Engineering second). Fortunately there were a lot of diagrams. The first diagram showed me what tools we needed: pliers, hammer, adjustable wrench, screwdriver.

That was when I ran into my first obstacle. You see, we don't have any tools at our house. We used to have tools, but then we had teenagers. And slowly the tools began to disappear. One was over at Danny's, another at Todd's. There were these vague promises to get them next time they were over there. But vague promises weren't going to tighten bolts and nuts.

It was scrounge time. I managed to find a pair of pliers in the utility drawer, under all the Mystery Parts left over from previous "some assembly required" toys. There was a bent screwdriver in the bathroom cabinet. I found the hammer in two parts, handle and claw, in the Mystery Drawer in the garage. The adjustable wrench was, er, um, uh, in the trunk of my car.

Will and I began assembling.

I got the seesaw together and held it up. "Yeah, it looks just like a seesaw," I said admiringly.

There was only one problem. It was all put together, but it wasn't on the swing. It was in my hands.

The engineering manual didn't mention the part about attaching the top bracket to the swing first. So I had to take the seesaw apart, hoist it over the top of the swing and then reassemble the bottom.

That was a regular occurrence on my assembly line. I didn't assemble a single part that I didn't have to go back at some point and disassemble.

Fortunately I had a lot of help from my five-year-old.

I would say, "Get me that metal part on the right." And Will would say, "Which one?" And I would remember that it is impossible to give directions to someone who doesn't know right from left.

I had the steps bolted to the slide part and was searching for the supporting legs when I turned around and found Will at the top of the ladder, preparing to slide down.

As I would get it together, he would play with it.

I assembled much of the swing set in the garage. I did figure out that, once I got the main frame partly assembled, I would be better off finishing that part outside rather than having a swing set permanently parked next to the van.

"Hey, Daddy, look at this," Will said, just as I was reading how Part 12-8 went inside Part 13-5 and right as I discovered that I had already bolted 13-5 to 14-9 using the hole where 12-8 went.

"Look, Daddy."

One quick glance "Uh-huh."

I was too preoccupied with finding Part 12-4 to give Will my full attention. Our weekend together was not quality time; it was just time.

As the day went on, it got colder and colder out. I would assemble pieces in the garage, away from the wind, then carry them out to put on the swing.

I would head back in and turn to see a lonely, shivering five-year-old, too cold to swing but too excited to give up and go in. So there he stood, pushing the swing seat back and forth.

By the time the sun was fading Sunday night, I had it all together except for the glider.

"I'll tell you what, Will," I said, nodding toward the growing darkness. "Let's finish up the glider next weekend."

"That's my favorite part," said Will, his face getting longer by the second.

It was back out to the garage, more fumbling and bolting. I was disassembling yet another section when I realized I hadn't heard a "Hey, Daddy, look" in quite a while. I started looking around. There he was in the corner, curled up with Part 15-18, this toy's Mystery Part, clutched in his hand.

The next day at work I was describing my lost weekend when one of the mothers I work with piped in: "You know, you can pay somebody to put a swing set together."

"You can?" I asked, rubbing my blistered fingers together.

"Yeah. They do it at Cycle World and they're real cheap."

I called and they charge thirty dollars to seventy dollars, depending on the swing set.

Letting someone else put together a swing set for you is cheap at any price.

CLOSING TIME

It's heading toward closing time so Ronnie heads back to the office to do the day's books.

He has a sign over his office door:

Authorized Personnel Only
If You're Bringing Money, You're Authorized

Inside the office is another sign:

BILL CLINTON'S 5 NEW IDEAS
1. Raise Taxes
2. Higher Taxes
3. Double Taxes
4. More Taxes
5. Added Taxes

"That's my wife's sign," says Ron.

Not that Ron disagrees with it.

"One of the biggest causes for small business failure is taxes. My first boss, Russ Casto, told me, if you go into business the first thing to do is hire a good accountant.

"The biggest reason that I'm not as profitable as I used to be: government taxes and insurance premiums. I furnish health insurance."

BEAT YESTERDAY

I've searched all my father's old papers and the one item I can't find is his old BEAT YESTERDAY book.

If you've ever owned a retail business you know what I'm talking about. The BEAT YESTERDAY books are logs that let you look back at the same day last year, the year before that, five years in the past, to see how sales today compare to sales on the same day a year ago.

I find them fascinating. My father would make little notations in his BEAT YESTERDAY book about the weather, any special events going on, any advertising he might have done.

Rain would explain why today's sales are so much lower than last year's sales. An ad in the newspaper might explain better sales.

Ronnie Matthews hasn't been beating yesterday as much as he would like to. "Sales have stayed about the same the last five years but I haven't lost any."

Chapter 13
Housewares
Department

MY WIFE THINKS HARDWARE-STORE CLERKS treat women differently than they do men. I tell her that from my experience they don't. My father never said, "Take advantage of all the women customers; they don't know what they're buying anyway." And Bob, one of the Loafers at Winfield Hardware, tells me that's one of the secrets to Ronnie Matthews's success. "He doesn't treat the women like idiots when they come in."

Women have invaded the Harvard Club, the IBM corporate boardroom, the New England Patriots locker room—all once men-only bastions. They have knocked down all the barriers of sex. Except one.

You will find more women in the locker room after the Super Bowl than in Winfield Hardware on this Thursday morning.

Or at least as many.

I have been counting all day at Winfield Hardware. One, two, three, four, five. . . . I am up to forty-eight in one column, but I am at eight in the other. Eight women customers today. Ronnie says there will be more on Saturday.

Women shop in hardware stores. But not as often as men. And not because they don't understand the inner workings of the double-hung door or the compression socket wrench.

Women strip furniture and replace furnace filters and even repair toilets. According to Data Resources, Inc., a research firm, 43 percent of do-it-yourselfers are women.

But women don't buy the equipment they need for those odd jobs at a hardware store as much as they do at discount stores like Wal-Mart and Target and at grocery stores. That's because they are in discount stores and supermarkets frequently. It's easier to pick up a hardware item then.

Ron estimates women make up about a quarter of his business. "Most of them are in to get paint. Not all. But most."

KIDDE HOME 5 FIRE EXTINGUISHER—$13.98

They call relief pitchers in baseball "firemen." That would have been an especially apt description of the first fire extinguisher.

It was closer to a baseball than to a modern squirt cylinder. Invented in 1734 by a German physician named Fuches, it was a bag full of glass balls, each filled with a mixture of salt and water. It actually looked like fun in the early ads: Entire families are pictured hurling the balls into a raging house fire.

Fun but really not all that effective. You'd need the entire National League to fight a medium-sized house fire.

In 1816 a British army captain named George Manby created a cylinder extinguisher from copper sheeting. It was two feet tall and held four gallons of liquid. Manby mixed three gallons of spigot water with pearl-ash then filled the remainder of the tank with compressed air. It worked. And soon the Hadley, Simkin & Lott store couldn't keep up with demand. But after fewer than a thousand were sold, the novelty wore off and no one bought any more. No one.

The design was revived fifty years later and boom—it was like a fire sale, so to speak.

5-Pound Bag Shredded Foam Rubber — $3.98

Once they finally figured out a way to use rubber, it was only a short hop to trying it every which way.

In 1929 E. A. Murphy, a scientist at Dunlop Latex Development Laboratories in England, got the idea to whip up rubber. Using an ordinary kitchen mixer he whipped latex up into a nice foam. He added a gel and the foam rubber could be poured into molds.

So what? you may say, which is pretty much what his coworkers said until they sat on the hardened foam rubber. Two years later they were using the foam rubber for motorcycle seats. The next year it was used for bus seats. Another couple of years and it was in mattresses.

Today it is everywhere.

This shredded variety is popular with craftspeople, who use it to fill pillows.

The Club — $29.98

My father would never have sold The Club at his hardware store. He always said he'd leave car parts to Western Auto. He said that until Western Auto started carrying hardware.

But now I find auto parts at many hardware stores and The Club at almost every hardware store. Who wouldn't want to sell a widely advertised item that has a built-in markup of 100 percent?

Thirty years ago there was no such thing as The Club.

There was also no such thing as carjacking and not a whole lot of grand theft auto.

James Winner, who has certainly fulfilled his surname destiny with this product, invented The Club to fill a need, a need for peace of mind when you park your car on the street.

Since he began marketing The Club in saturation TV commercials in 1986, his company, Winner International, has sold over 13 million!

Winner, who is from Pittsburgh, got the idea for The Club after his Cadillac was stolen in the early 1980s. Since he wasn't mechanically inclined—he had spent most of fifty-four years selling chemicals and women's clothing—he engaged Charles Johnson, a Cleveland mechanic, to fashion his invention. And herein lies the bone of contention. Johnson, through his attorneys, claimed he wasn't just the hired hand, that he was a partner. The suit was settled out of court with Winner paying Johnson a reported $10 million.

The first Club was nothing more than a crude bar with a padlock on it. But it worked, in the sense that any would-be car thief needed to carry some serious chain-cutter to foil The Club.

What really kick-started sales of The Club was a TV commercial with Sharon, Pennsylvania, policeman John Klaric. In the ad Klaric declared, "I'm not an actor, I'm a policeman," and went on to endorse The Club. At this writing Klaric is no longer doing the commercials—he stopped in a dispute over compensation.

The Club has given much fodder to comedians and sitcoms. Once on his late-night talk show David Letterman locked up his golf cart with The Club. Another time Letterman quipped that NASA should have used The Club on the lost space probe.

Winner International just laughs all the way to the bank.

The company, which had only three employees in 1986, now has one hundred eighty plus a sales force of sixty. In 1992 Winner International earned $30 million on sales of $100 million. That same year the company sold 3.1 million units of The Club at a suggested retail price of $59.95. Good money for a metal stick with a lock in it.

12-Ounce Can WD-40—$1.98

What would life be like without WD-40?
Squeakier.
Stickier.
Creakier.
There'd be more stuck doors and squeaky drawers and creaky floors.

But we don't have to worry about that because there is WD-40, has been since 1953.

WD-40, like Velcro and duct tape, is one of those happy accidents of industry. The Rocket Chemical Company (honest, that was the name), now the WD-40 Company, was searching for a chemical that would prevent corrosion on airplanes and rockets and eliminate moisture from electrical circuitry when WD-40 was invented. The name came from the oil's purpose, water displacement, and the number of formulas that Rocket Chemical's laboratory went through before it came up with just the right one—40. Thus Water Displacement Formula 40, or WD-40 for short.

But that's just the beginning of the WD-40 story.

As engineers are wont to do, the guys at Rocket Chemical began surreptitiously taking the stuff home, trying it out on other projects. They discovered it would unstick locks, desqueak doors, free up rusted nuts. It was better than petroleum jelly at freeing up tiny hands that somehow got stuck inside the cookie jar.

Rocket Chemical began selling its all-purpose lubricant to hardware stores in 1958 and in 1993 sales topped $100 million. A spokeswoman for WD-40 says market research has demonstrated that WD-40 is in more households than any other branded product: 79 percent of U.S. homes, almost four of five, have a spray can of WD-40 somewhere in the garage or utility drawer.

Homeowners know that when all else fails, WD-40 works.

Although the label on the can lists its uses as "lubrication, rust prevention and moisture displacement," WD-40 fans have found their own uses, and the WD-40 Company has a file of letters to prove it:

Fishermen claim WD-40, when sprayed on bait, attracts fish.

Dog owners swear it cures mange.

Birdlovers say they spray it on metal birdhouse poles and it keeps squirrels from climbing into birdhouses.

Sun worshipers say its frees up trouser zippers that stick in salt air.

The Denver police claim to have extracted a nude burglar who had wedged himself into a vent at a café by spraying him with a large dose of WD-40.

The WD-40 Company even has a letter in its files from eighty-two-year-old Glenn Palmer of Mission, Texas: "I spray it on my hips and knees. It keeps my joints limber; that way I can go dancing two or three nights a week."

10-POUND BAG OL' DIZ CHARCOAL BRIQUETTES— $4.98

Henry Ford didn't invent charcoal as you may have heard. He just figured out a way to compact the charcoal from his factories into briquettes that were perfect for backyard barbecuing.

Charcoal makers—called charcoal burners, by their friends—were around in the 1700s, making charcoal, which was used for making iron, gunpowder, printers ink, black paint. People even used it to clean their teeth. Ugh.

Charcoal burners were different. They lived a solitary existence that revolved around building a mound of wood, sod, and mud some thirty feet high and then burning it, perhaps for a month or more. While this burning was going on, the charcoal maker lived every minute next to the mound, sleeping fitfully, afraid that a flame might erupt and then explode into a fire that would destroy his mound. They didn't even bathe, not that that was so unusual in the nineteenth century (or with my twelve-year-old son in summer).

Charcoal burners were as much craftsmen as silversmiths. It was an art, building the mound, lighting it, keeping the flame just right so that in the end the mound would collapse on itself. A burner would even have to know how to climb the mound, to patch over a flame, without getting burned or falling into the furnace inside.

When it was all burned down perfectly, he would shovel it into barrels and cart it to the city, singing "Charcoal by the bushel, charcoal by the peck, charcoal by the frying pan, or anyway you lek." Did I mention that in addition to poor personal habits they also weren't so hot with rhyme?

ELECTRIC FOOD DEHYDRATOR, BEEF JERKY MACHINE, AND YOGURT MAKER—$29.98

My father wouldn't have allowed a Veg-O-Matic within a city block of his hardware store. He hated the little geegaws and thingamajiggies that salesmen were always pitching him. He called them junk.

Every now and then he'd give in and add a new miracle glue or a medium-tech four-in-one tool. But the out-and-out carnival inventions were just plain out.

But Winfield Hardware has the Veg-o-Matic and the

Electric Food Dehydrator, Beef Jerky Machine, and Yogurt Maker. Ron stocks the occasional junk item. "Hey, if it sells . . ." is his motto.

Two companies dominate the junk-product market: Popeil and Ronco. And—this is probably no surprise—they are pretty much the same, both founded by Ron Popeil.

Ron Popeil is a modern-day medicine man who rolls into town—via the TV airwaves—with a smooth line and rolls out before people figure out what hit them. I mean who really needs to scramble their eggs inside the shell or vacuum their records?

The original Ronco product, the Veg-O-Matic, was invented by Ron's father, Sam. And Ron's late-night TV commercials gave the world the catchphrase "It slices, it dices . . ."

In his thirty years in business the fifty-nine-year-old Popeil has sold more than $1 billion worth of his products, most of which were pitched on TV and wound up in hardware and dime stores a few years later.

Ron Popeil didn't create the "I've fallen and I can't get up" Medic Alert gizmo and he didn't invent the Clapper that lets you turn off the lights with a little applause. But he wishes he had. And he invented the marketing techniques that make them possible: screaming announcers yelling "But wait! There's more!" and "If you act now!" and "Order before midnight, so you don't forget!"

It's the 1990s and Ron Popeil is still hawking his incredible inventions. (He invents most everything he sells.) His latest is the GLH Formula Number 9 Hair System, nicknamed Hair in a Can by anyone who has seen the commercial.

It's like powdering your hair—and scalp—so it seems that you have more hair than you really do. It's cheaper than the Hair Club for Men and it comes in a can! Incidentally, GLH stands for "Great Looking Hair" and comes in nine amazing hues. In its first six months on the market Popeil sold more than 450,000 cans of GLH at $39.92.

And Ronnie Matthews swears it will never end up on the shelves of Winfield Hardware. "Maybe if it sliced and diced . . ."

Chapter 14
Closing Time

It's closing time for America's hardware stores. Six o'clock. The last customers have filed out of Winfield Hardware. There's no "last-chance" fellow begging for Ronnie to stay open five more minutes so he can pick up that last item he needs to finish his job. "Not that I haven't had a few of those in my time," Ronnie says, and chuckles.

Ronnie turns off the light, double-checks the back door, and shuffles out. He locks the door of Winfield Hardware for the 5,212th time.

"See ya tomorrow," he says. Not to me or to John or to Kenny. But to the store.

See ya tomorrow, Winfield Hardware.

•   •   •

My father locked the door on his hardware store for the last time on August 5, 1984, my thirty-seventh birthday. I was there and took a snapshot.

After thirty-two years in business he walked away.

He didn't seem sad. I was the one who insisted on taking a picture.

He seemed relieved. A weight removed.

There was probably more in the look on his face than I realized at the time. Because within two years my father was dead.

The last four years had been hard ones for him. His business lost money all four years—the first time he had lost money since his first year in hardware.

At the time he attributed it to the fact that he wasn't there all the time. He went in only a couple of hours a day those years.

But before he died, he told me what happened. It's an old story: employee theft. You can't spend your adult life placing Bibles in motel rooms and not be hurt when a trusted employee takes advantage of your absence.

My father never tried to push me into the family business. He was glad he could provide me a summer job while I was in college. But he knew I was going to college because I didn't want to spend the rest of my life in retail.

He talked to me about taking over twice. Once in 1974—I was coming off a two-game losing streak: A magazine I founded had failed and a political candidate I worked for had lost. I was broke and back home. He told me he had been approached about opening a hardware store in Colonial Heights, a southern suburb of my hometown. He would do it if I wanted to run it. I told him no. I still had things to prove to myself.

Ten years later, as he negotiated to sell his hardware store, he asked me one last time. "If you don't want it, I'm going to sell it," he said. It was harder to say no this time, to turn down a successful business. But by then I was established as a writer, established in a distant town, with a family. I swallowed hard, but again I said no.

He never did sell the store. The people who wanted to buy it couldn't come up with the money.

In the end he had a going-out-of-business sale. He netted about a fourth of what his inventory was worth.

My father died in 1986, a hardware man to the end.

One of his favorite stories was from the *Saturday Evening Post*, a 1964 morality tale that author John O'Hara called "The Hardware Man." It was set in 1928, the year before the Great Depression, and it was about the competition between two Gibbsville, Pennsylvania, hardware stores, one clinging to the old ways, the other winning by adopting new marketing strategies.

"Honest value, good merchandise, that's what we were founded on and no tricks," promised Tom Esterly, the owner of Esterly Bros. Est. 1859, the old-line hardware store.

My father knew all about tricks. He knew all about bigger competitors trying to starve out the little guys. When he opened his hardware store, the only people selling hardware were hardware stores. When he closed three decades later, everyone was selling hardware, from the supermarkets to the service stations.

He used to say that Kmart sold it cheaper than he could buy it.

Once a landlord refused to renew his lease so he could open his own hardware store in the building. It failed. And when he offered his leftover stock to my father at a reduced price, my father declined. Politely, but he declined.

Still he survived.

Ronnie Matthews and Winfield Hardware are survivors. "The only thing that keeps us going is service. Big Bear doesn't thread pipe or sharpen blades." Ronnie is talking about the local supermarket, which sells traditional hardware items, from electrical tape to eye bolts.

Ronnie doesn't see a bright future for the small hardware store. "I think the days of small retailers are marked. The people with money are gonna win."

Ronnie isn't alone in this belief. According to a survey by *Hardware Age,* 71 percent of hardware-store owners say their chief competition is a discount store, usually Wal-Mart, followed by Kmart. When Ronnie Matthews talks about the people with money, this is who he means.

These giant discounters carry anywhere from fifty thousand to one hundred thousand items, where the average hardware store stocks some eight thousand to eighteen thousand different items. Hardware stores see discount stores as public enemy number one because of price competition and because they cherry-pick lines, carrying the most profitable items and leaving the merchandise with thin profit margins to the hardware stores.

This has forced many hardware stores to get back to basics, what they have always done best: service. They cut glass, they make keys, they put together bikes, mix paint, even go out and fix windows.

HWI, which is Ronnie Matthews's buying group, has a two-day seminar to show its members how to take advantage of having a Wal-Mart in the area. They stress it is a seminar to teach not how to compete but how to take advantage. That means expanding product selection, especially in plumbing, electrical, and builders' hardware, and improving customer relations. That doesn't mean putting a greeter at the door Wal-Mart style. It means doing what Ronnie Matthews has always done: serving your customers.

And instead of fighting the discount stores on screwdrivers and pliers, they advise store owners to beef up the bolt section and carry every imaginable fastener.

Squeezing hardware stores from the other side are the giant home improvement centers, the HQs and the Home Depots and the Furrows.

The typical Home Depot is one hundred thousand

square feet and carries thirty thousand to thirty-five thousand different items. *The Wall Street Journal* credits the spartan surroundings, the rafter ceilings and concrete floors, with enabling the company to undercut hardware-store prices by 20 percent.

The average ticket at a hardware store is twelve dollars; at a home improvement center it's thirty-six dollars. It's easy to explain that difference. Hardware stores sell lots of small items. Home improvement centers also add big-ticket items—lumber, floor model power tools, doors, windows—into the mix.

Chris Vroom (what a wonderful last name), of the Chicago investment firm Alex Brown & Sons, predicts that by the year 2000, 40 percent of all hardware and building materials will be sold by Home Depot and Lowe's.

To fight the Home Depots, hardware stores are looking for niches: outdoor power equipment, high-end decorative hardware, repair shops, top-of-the-line lawnmowers, brass andirons and tool sets for fireplaces, gas logs.

Do hardware stores have a future?

There were 29,148 hardware stores in 1939, the year my mother and father were married, according to the 1946 Department of Commerce publication *Establishing and Operating a Hardware Store*. In 1955, the year my father opened his first hardware store, *Changing Times* magazine estimated there were 35,000 hardware stores. By 1994 there were 29,388, according to American Business Information.

This is not a dynamic industry, for sure. Fast-food restaurant figures for that same sixty-five-year period would blow you away.

But no one ever said the hardware industry is dynamic. What it is is steady.

And hardware stores continue to increase their sales, breaking records at a steady, if not record-breaking clip. In January 1992 hardware stores did a record $1.211 billion worth of business, eclipsing the record month of June 1990, when hardware retailers did $1.141 billion in sales.

The average hardware store did $408,329 in sales in 1993. That's a lot of screws at $1.19 a box.

Hardware-store sales totaled more than $12 billion in 1993. For comparison, liquor stores had sales of about $19 billion that same year.

The hardware store that stays in business for five years has a life expectancy of about twenty-five years, according to government studies. That's about as long as one person can put up with the hassles and headaches of small-business ownership.

I don't think the hardware store is ready just yet for the endangered-species list. In fact, I think there will be hardware stores as long as there are do-it-yourselfers and Saturday morning handymen, as long as people like to gather and talk about their homes, as long as people want to remodel and renovate. And as long as people live in neighborhoods. It's just not economically feasible to build a home improvement center on every corner. And it's not an efficient use of precious Saturday morning time to drive ten miles to save a dollar on your purchase of a pound of nails and a tube of caulk.

But the neighborhood hardware store is about more than time management and cost consciousness anyway.

It's about patronizing a place where you know folks and where folks know you.

And as long as there is someone willing to run it, the friendly neighborhood hardware store will survive.

Last time I was back in my hometown, I made a journey to my father's old hardware store. Of course it's no longer a hardware store. It's Ware Well Clothing, a low-priced dress shop. But I could still see the faded "Munford Do It Yourself Store" painted on the brick front, now mostly hidden by the Ware Well Clothing sign.

The smell is gone. In a decade they have wiped out the aroma of hardware: of lubricating oil and spilled paint and sawdust. It now reeks of fabric dye and inexpensive perfume.

I didn't feel sadness. I didn't want to cry.

But I felt something. I'd been in that old building too many times before not to feel something. What I felt was my father. He'd spent more waking hours of his life in that old brick shell than he had in our house. This was his home.

There were a few scars left from his three decades: faded spots on the floor where his fixtures used to be. Here's where paint used to be. There were hand tools. How many bags of concrete mix did I stack in the front window?

The clerk watched me with a puzzled look. They probably don't get many men looking for cheap women's dresses.

"May I help you?" she asked.

May I help you? How many times has that phrase been uttered in this building? Thousands? Millions?

I scanned the aisles, looking for any other signs of my father's life. They'd repainted the walls, the air-conditioner, the bathrooms.

"What used to be here?" I asked her.

She shook her head, furrowed her brow, and paused. "I think, a hardware store."

Acknowledgments

THE AVERAGE HOUSE in this country is thirty years old. That means the average house in this country is in need of repair! And on an almost constant basis. That makes this the greatest time in history for hardware and do-it-yourself.

And for a book about hardware and do-it-yourself.

Many people contributed to this book—I just wish a few more of them had been willing to research and type and edit and rewrite. I had to do all that stuff myself.

Virtually everything I know about hardware and hardware stores I learned from my father and from my next-door neighbor Walter Shankel.

My father never kept any secrets from me about his hardware store. In fact, after he died I told my mother a few things that he had never shared with her. She never knew the reason he and his longtime partner broke up, she didn't know that his store had lost money the last four years in business, she didn't know about other problems in his business. He shared these things with me, but he protected her.

Walter Shankel has always been like a second father to me. My parents got married in 1939 and moved to the big city (Kingsport, Tennessee, qualifies only in comparison to the farms they grew up on). They rented a room from Walter and his wife Herb and for the next forty-seven years—until my father died—the Statens and the Shankels lived either in the same house or next door to each other. My mother still lives next to the Shankels.

My father worked six days a week in his hardware store so he had little time—or inclination, I must admit—for doing handyman jobs around the house. Walter worked shift work that included long weekends off. He was always puttering around, fixing things, building things, remodeling things. He added a carport, stairs for an apartment, a brick barbecue grill. He taught me more about the uses of hardware than my father. I only wish I had been a better pupil. Some people are just not meant to drive a nail straight.

That's why I'm the writer of this book. I'm a better writer than I am a plumber.

The hundred or so men and the two women who worked in my father's hardware store over the three decades he was open all taught me something. I've forgotten some of their names. But I've never forgotten them.

Thanks to Ronnie Matthews for opening up his hardware store and his thought processes. If you're ever in the Huntington area of West Virginia stop in and sit a spell, listen to what The Loafer's Club is up to.

My brother-in-law Powell Toth steered me to Ronnie and provided all the necessary introductions. And several good stories.

Many industry representatives helped with the history of hardware. Among them: Jack Merry of the American Plywood Association, Rochelle Friedman Walk of Dutch Boy, Jan Healy of Rust-Oleum, the folks at the National Hardware Show. There were others who never told me their names.

Thanks to the staff at the Louisville Free Public Library, particularly Claudia, who is like my own personal librarian.

Here's that paragraph of endless names that authors love to include, in no particular order: David Jenkins, Larry Magnes, John Markel, Bob Francis, Chris Klapheke, David Vish, Jayne McClew, Tim Furnish, Kate Buford, Dyan Welsh, Bob Sokoler, Kirby Adams, John Moreman, Sheri Arnett, Jim Reed, Mary Caldwell, Chris Wohlwend, Jena Monohan, Pat McDonogh, Geri McDonogh, Greg Johnson, Ronni Lundy, David Inman,

Walter Chapin, Melinda Pomeroy, Al Futtrell, Chris Davis, Ed Cetera.

Thanks to my wife, Judy, who may be happier than I am that this book is finished.

Thanks to Gary Luke, the editor on my last book, who told me he liked the idea for this one on the same day he told me he was leaving Simon & Schuster. And to David Dunton, who was the interim editing shepherd, until he left publishing for rock and roll. And finally to Bob Mecoy, who was responsible for bringing this thing in.

Well, here it is.

A couple of notes of caution: Don't head to Winfield Hardware for a piece of glass. Ronnie Matthews no longer cuts glass. Nor does he sell linoleum or Formica. And he doesn't carry The Club or Ronco's Food Dehydrator.

I included those and a few other items because I see them at other hardware stores. And because I like them. Ronnie's store is typical, but no hardware store can be completely typical of the industry.

And don't use the prices in this book as a shopping guide. They were correct at the time of writing but in the retail arena prices can change at any moment, depending on supply, demand, and the cost of raw materials. Prices may vary. Void where prohibited. Licensed drivers only.

About the Author

NOTHING REALLY TO DO WITH HARDWARE . . .
. . . But if You're Curious About the Writer Fellow

I didn't always want to be a writer.

I wish I could say I did. There are some great romantic legends about aspiring young writers: hawking their penny papers to friends, scribbling feverishly in their diaries, taking notes on the eccentrics of the neighborhood.

But I didn't set out to be a writer.

No, originally I wanted to be a cowboy.

I was greatly influenced by Matt Dillon and Paladin.

It sounded great: ride a horse, camp out under the stars, never take a bath.

Then I discovered something that would preclude me from ever riding the range: I was afraid of cows.

My next career goal was to become a major league baseball player. Obviously that was a lot of years and a lot of pounds ago. It's been so long since I wanted to be an athlete that I don't even pronounce it ath-a-lete anymore.

I was just sure I was going to be the next Yogi Berra.

Then I met a kid who could throw a curveball. If you've never tried to hit a curveball, let me tell you this about it: It is not an optical illusion.

That's when I decided to become a writer.

I wish I could say my decision was influenced by my readings of Emerson or Thoreau or Joyce. But it wasn't. I read them because my teachers made me read them. I was most influenced by a writer that no one ever mentions anymore. His books are all out of print. I'm not sure he was technically even a writer. I know when he was young he played drums in several big bands. He wrote gags for many of the great comedians, from Ed Wynn to Jerry Lewis. But he was in his fifties before his first book was published.

His name was Jack Douglas and he's dead now. But I think he's the funniest writer who ever lived. His stuff does to me what George Burns did to Jack Benny. Burns cracked Benny up just by clearing his throat. Douglas can send me into a giggling fit with a simple aside.

Douglas taught me something: I didn't know writers were allowed to be funny. Comic books were funny. Books were, well, serious.

I bought my first Douglas book strictly because of the title: *My Brother Was an Only Child*. It was a collection of savage satires, nonsensical stories, left-field one-liners, and fables that would make Aesop blush. It was the wildest thing my eighth-grade eyes had ever encountered. There was Chapter 19: "To hell with chapter 19. Every damn book you pick up has a chapter 19." There was Chapter 47: "Songs I Learned at My Mother's Knee and Other Locations." And there was the Epilogue: "This book is bound in Old Moroccan leather. So if your Old Moroccan grandfather is missing. . . ."

Douglas followed it with *Never Trust a Naked Bus Driver; A Funny Thing Happened to Me on the Way to the Grave,* his autobiography; and a series of burlesques about life in New England with his Japanese-American wife and their pet wolves. The New England epistles were funny but he never recaptured the pure absurdist spirit of his first three books.

I remember taking my paperback copy of *My Brother Was an Only Child* on a trip to my aunt Ida's. My aunt Ida didn't have any kids of her own so she always doted on me. I was reading and cracking up at Jack Douglas, so when I set the book down, she picked it up and started reading. She had read maybe ten pages when she looked up at me and said, "You know, I think this man's a communist."

I didn't even know what a communist was, but I knew Jack Douglas had written some pretty powerful words if they could rile up my aunt Ida.

That's when I knew I wanted to be a writer.